The Boy in the Chicken Coop

The

Untold Stories of Trauma

Done unto the Young Men of Our Society

and

The Addictions That Sweep Them Away

Steven B. Sherman, LMHC

For Lori

Dedication

This book is dedicated to the wives, moms, dads, brothers, sisters, grandparents, aunts, and uncles of the many men who walk among us in despair, within the abyss that *is* addiction and trauma. Their continuing support and hopefulness is nothing short of uncompromising love, forgiveness and compassion.

Most of all, this book is dedicated and is a tribute to all the men who have shared their heartfelt stories with me. Their resiliency, their capacity for survival, and their raw ability to try and try and try again will forever be etched in my expanding consciousness. I witness lost modesty and a state of the most humble in each and every encounter.

The Boy in the Chicken Coop

CONTENTS

Foreword

For almost half of my life, I've worked in the human service field, beginning with adults with different abilities (formerly *disabilities*) who were diagnosed with autism or any number of varying pathologies and deficits along the autistic spectrum, including mental retardation with features of obsessive-compulsive disorder, Asperger's syndrome, and Prater-Willi syndrome, to name a few. I've also worked on a suicide hot line, befriending those who have chosen to end their lives. For the last five years, I've had a focus on addiction counseling with men. My work has primarily taken place within a Section 35 facility, which means that these men were civilly committed by a court of law to address their addictive lifestyles and the dire consequences that come with them.

What I began to notice in my work with these men was that at least eighty five percent of them had become addicted to some substance or variety of substances (e.g., heroin, alcohol, oxycontin, etc.) because of traumatic events that had occurred at some point in their lives. Some of the men were aware of these events, while some had not perceived such events as traumatic because of how often and how early in life they occurred. Repetition has a funny way of normalizing or *patterning* both behaviors and events throughout a life. After a while we don't notice the pain because we get numb to the experience as well as the emotional consequences.

At this time my studies in neuroscience, consciousness, and brain function accelerated through my work utilizing a process known as Brainwave Optimization (BWO). This process uses electroencephalographic (EEG) technology combined with computer analysis to identify dominant or stuck brainwaves or frequencies. (When neurons communicate with one another, they produce electrical currents or frequencies.) Through this work I am able to see the potential brainwave correlates of brain imbalance that often result in the residual effects of traumatic experiences. My knowledge was further enhanced by the esteemed works of Dr. Oliver Sacks, Dr. V. S. Ramachandran, Dr. Robert Scaer, Dr. Stephen Porges, Dr. David Berceli, Dr. Eric Kandel, Dr. Peter Levine, and Dr. Bessel A. van der Kolk, to name but a few, who all are at the top of their fields in neuroscience, memory, and trauma.

Through the unfortunate experiences of their clients, these doctors have all applied their remarkable clinical observations and detective-like inquisitiveness to coalesce a picture of trauma that transcends the mind and reveals the brain as an organ of habit and, per Dr. Michael Shermer, *patternistic* in its' behavior. The brain is considered by many to be the seat of all experience, the organ that makes the body move. Percepts translate into concepts and beliefs; actions flow converting these abstract bodily functions into our lifestyles and expectations, and decisions and ultimately, the outcomes and conclusions of our lives.

I made the commitment to write this book as a way to communicate and distill my observations and understanding of trauma as it manifests through the addictive and destructive life *choices*, if that is indeed what we can call them, of the men whom I have served. Their stories continue to reveal a deeply personal and troubling trend of abuse at the hands of parents, grandparents, brothers, sisters, and cousins. This list could also include aunts, uncles, and family friends, all of whom have contributed gravely to the troubled, imbalanced brains that guide these men through their days and nights, in and out of court rooms, prisons, and meetings with their probation or parole officers and other relationships which too often prove destructive or threatening.

It is my hope that, by sharing their stories and my understanding of the science of trauma and the implication of addiction, I can help the reader understand those men who walk among us in shame and confusion and who wallow in existences marked by chronic homelessness, profound dissolution, loneliness, isolation, and fear.

Respectfully, *SBS*

Every night and every morn
Some to misery are born.
Every morn and every night
Some are born to sweet delight.
Some are born to sweet delight,
Some are born to endless night.

—William Blake, *Auguries of Innocence*

A Mother's Plea

"I do want you to know that the last time my son was committed he ran away the day he was to be released. His plan was to take cough syrup and cough tablets then go sit on the train track and wait for a train to hit him. He had said that he knew that I didn't want him back in my home like this and he was sick of treatment centers and that he wanted to die. This is what I am very afraid of happening. I love my son, please help...!!"

Jason's Letter

Jason presented with alcohol (*ETOH* in medical terminology) abuse issues and had been referred to our facility Men's Addiction Treatment Center, on a Section 35 commitment, meaning that he was court mandated to receive treatment in our secure inpatient facility for a period of up to thirty days, which is really a rough estimate of the rather arbitrary length of stay. This commitment process is typically imposed when an individual loses the ability to make choices in his or her best interest and whose choices often infringe upon others. The patient's drinking or drugging habit is out of his or her control and presents a risk to the patient or to others.

Although Jason was referred due to his abuse of alcohol, it quickly became clear that he had an extensive history of traumatic events, of which I only began to glimpse through his thoughtful and trusted sharing. We call this a co-occurring disorder, or comorbidity, when substance abuse or dependence occurs along with other psychiatric concerns such as anxiety, depression, post traumatic stress, etc. Jason's twin brother had committed suicide five years earlier, and for the five years since, Jason had isolated himself in his home, had not been able to work, and had drunk heavily and incessantly. In the literal sense of the word, he had dissociated from this world and would often be found in places of which he had no recollection. A complete and total blackout, a collapsing of *personal* reality.

For an example of this collapsing of *personal* reality, at times Jason had been found walking along the highway, having driven and subsequently abandoned his car; had been picked up and questioned by police; and had been returned to his home substance free, sober, and unable to account for his whereabouts.

Jason would often feel extremely frightened from seemingly having no power, no recollection, no personal agency, and no control or *personal* involvement over his actions. At some point he had gotten into his car and driven but had a total amnesia of time, place, person, and even purpose or motivation. He felt guilty for putting his wife and family through such terror and shame for living his life in such an unaccountable way. According to Jason's telling, both he and his brother had experienced similar brutality and would often dissociate or mentally relocate together, leaving their present reality behind temporarily. They would conjoin and, through mysterious and dynamic neurological processes little understood, arrive at or construct a safer, more habitable *abode* or inner space that was not to be seen or known to anyone but them.

Here is a letter Jason wrote to help me understand his very private and very personal experience:

Noises, lights and sights

You pierce my thoughts and shake my mind, body and vision. You steal my peace and rock my heart. I can't stand what you do to me! You fracture my present with flashes from my past. I relive scenes from long ago...the beatings: horror and terror. I hear my mother's demonic voice, it echo's in my head: "I hate you...I wish I never had you...you are dirty and I will kill you before you kill me!" The ripping of my hair; the tearing of my skin; the screaming in the night— blood curdling screaming—that rips and tears through my mind. I hang onto my other half (Adam) as we disappear— we go to a place where warm fuzzies surround us and we are cradled ever so sweetly. We laugh and play with the faith of a child...a faith in knowing that we are safe, we are going to survive together. We'll be okay.

Flinching and jolting like bursts of electric current coursing through my body; it hurts me physically and destroys my peace of mind. It reminds me of watching my mother line up items on the bed and making us choose which one she would beat us with. The anticipation of what's to come sends a flood of terror through my body...The bashings with the vacuum cleaner, sticking my fingers into the blender as she turns it on. Smashing my head into the refrigerator door. The snapping of the belt before the buckle left its welt —all come rushing back when I hear the noises that match.

I am riddled with what seem to be uncontrollable reactions and responses to these noises, lights and sights. I am trying ever so hard to reframe my associations between noises and reality...this current reality. I am holding on; gripping ever so tightly to reality. Sometimes I feel like I'm cracking into pieces. Shards of who I am go crashing to the floor. I see the pieces of my life lying there on the floor, scattered amongst a pool of cool, sticky blood. In the reflections of these mirrored pieces, I see my brother, Adam, looking back at me. The alcohol and substitutes I jam into my body burns me to the core. The more I remember, the more I drink; trying to drown out the noises, lights and sights —trying to drown out the voice of God, as my conscience rings ever so loudly in my head...reminding me of right and wrong. I drink to disappear, to forget, to die.

My blackouts now are increasing daily. I'm losing more and more time. I see my brother, he holds my hand. I feel his warmth as he calls to me: "Everything is okay now." I do not remember. I do not feel. I disappear into the night. I leave everything behind me and morph into nothingness. I am one again. I am whole with the one that completes me; two parts that make the one. I am strong now, nothing can touch me. I slip away into a void where happiness and joy abound. It must be this, for I don't remember. I come to...without any scars; without any pain; without any memory. The shards of my life shining within the light are no longer drowning in cool puddles of sticky blood. I come to and for a brief moment... I'm in paradise. I hold onto it ever so tightly before it all rushes back again. I slip into the night and fade to gray.

This is an all-too-common story, which casually but inevitably drips from the unsettled, quivering lips of young men whose lives have been sold to addiction and prostituted out to the momentary euphoria of its promise: the wretched space between what's real and the avoided truths of their emotional lives.

The story that Jason tells is true in its most grotesque sense, and yet it barely scrapes the surface of its deep and penetrating impact upon a developing child—the child that he was—and a developing young man and his identical twin brother who, sadly, had taken his own life some five years prior to our meeting.

These two men—boys really, brothers in pain,endured the neurophysiological, psychophysiological, and emotional repercussions of extreme fear and physical torture at the hands of their alcoholic mother, whose hatred of them manifested in ways so utterly despicable and hideous that to speak of them with words could never qualify the brothers' anguish and undeniable terror. These loving, bonded brothers developed what is known as dissociative identity disorder (DID), in which a person's brain perceives external events as life threatening and, as a pervasive and enduring state of helplessness descends upon him or her, a flood of neurophysiological processes establishes new perceptual models for coping, creating new schemas and constructs of an external/internal world. Unique personalities arose to maintain simple existence, to survive; Their psyches split and fragmented into broken parts of the whole, simply to maintain that living essence. A sort of quasi-existence.

I had the quite humbling and frightening experience of meeting one of those *constructed* identities or new perceptual models that was being used to cope, a very unique personality who had emerged from the fractured psyche of Jason. *He* approached me one day and, by his mannerisms, the way he walked, how he held himself in pride and force and intensity, strength of character and how he spoke, I could tell at once this was not Jason but without a doubt some other personality; someone new had arrived wearing Jason's skin.

Under so-called normal or everyday conditions and with Jason himself (the host person as it is sometimes referred to), there would be a constant fear and nervousness, a restless agitation about all activity going on around him. Doors simply closing would cause great consternation. He would be visibly shaken and begin to tremble at the chirp, chirp, chirp sound of door alarms resetting. Jason would constantly and rapidly blink his eyes as if something were about to happen.

The awful anticipation of pain creates a hyperstartle response, which is the result of a state of internal hyper-reactivity, a highly aroused sympathetic nervous system and occurs in many people who have post-traumatic stress disorder. They become so extremely sensitive to their surroundings that they literally hear everything or become hyper-aware of every little noise or action going on around them. This is survival in its most primitive, most pure and alluring state.

When I was approached by this *other* presence, this other personality, those original, daily features of fear had completely vanished. Doors could slam shut, people could shout, and door alarms could reset, and there *he* would be: upright, stoic, solid, strong, and physically capable of defending and protecting or manhandling anyone who would foolishly dare to intrude upon Jason. Any threat, real or imagined, that might befall Jason would be met with force: a head butt to the nose or a firm hand to the throat as I had seen firsthand in an explosive and prodigious reaction. There had been a conversion of sorts from a gentle and fearful being to an archetypal warrior born from both brain structure and subjective experience.

He was a force unto himself harnessing power and strength, purpose and intention. We spoke at great length, and as we did, I began to understand what his role was, why *he* existed at all. He had a well-defined mission. His job, as he told me with great precision and passion, was to "*protect the boy*" (referring to Jason), nothing else. This was his sole purpose; *he* had been created or born or evolved and manifested for this purpose alone. He would emerge at the first sign of possible infringement toward Jason. Jason would fade into the background of consciousness and out would arise this phantasmal *other* to serve and protect, to ensure safety and life.

It is at once horrifying and awesome to bear witness to such an intrusion upon someone's *original* consciousness or personality, his or her particular set of characteristics, traits and mental wanderings and physical capacities—the self. To be selected (to choose perhaps an applicable phrase of Darwinism here) by natural pressures to hone or fabricate such a defense as this in order to allow an organic system, brothers in this case, their continued survival is a marvel of our species. It is a fantastic achievement of the human brain, perhaps a natural and as of yet, an undefined *law* on the one hand, and an unfortunate necessity for survival on the other.

The narratives that fill these pages are true to the lives and circumstances they describe, and many are of similar intensity, but thankfully, the brains, the physiology, and the psyches of few men have created such desperate adaptations (or exaptations, as they are also known) for the sake of survival. For Jason, the challenge of living his life, or attempting to do so the only way he knows how, without his other half would be unimaginable. Especially for those of us who do not coexist or co-inhabit as a twin. Jason not only expresses great emotional turbulence, a sense of utter displacement for the loss of his beloved brother, as if two soldiers from battle, but he is also forced to confront himself without half of his soul, half of his flesh, half of his knowing, half of his biological inheritance, an incompleteness of association. Jason experiences what is commonly referred to as *missing twin syndrome*, in which one is displaced without the other. The searchlight will forever be cast, penetrating the visual, emotional, and psychic landscapes for that integral piece of the individual that eludes his or her current daily reality.

***

Often, life comes at us with such unpredictable force and is so tremendously overwhelming that the brain, in concert with the nervous system, must find a way to cope, to ensure that of all the systems of the body can function as a whole and continue to do so. The brain is the control center for our entire body—command central, if you will. It controls every cell, every organ, every tissue, and the entire autonomic nervous system (composed of the sympathetic and parasympathetic nervous systems), as well as reactions to stress and behaviors and the endocrine system. The entire contents of the body are commanded and regulated by the brain. The brain is in fact an integral part of the nervous system. It, along with the spinal cord, are the first parts of our human anatomy to grow in utero. Skeletal components and organs are built around this structure.

The right and left or bi-lateral Temporal lobes may in fact have robust connections to the autonomic nervous system. A process called Brainwave Optimization developed by Lee Gerdes of Brainstate Technologies, which I used extensively for five years working with people who had been experiencing chronic depression, debilitating anxiety, post traumatic stress even chronic pain demonstrated this possibility. In brief, through this process brainwaves or frequencies were observed through an electroencephalograph [EEG], and computer analysis to identify those brainwaves which appeared to be out of balance: in excess or diminished, in the Temporal and other lobes. When an acoustic mirroring process (tones which were of the same frequency of the out of balance or dominant brainwaves), was used to reflect back to the brain (through headphones) those same frequencies, the brain changed itself to reduce or increase those frequencies. The result was a reduction and often elimination of their symptoms.   Chronic pain was no longer a primary experience.   The nightmares and flashbacks typically associated with post traumatic stress were gone. Symptoms of anxiety, depression and arousal of the sympathetic nervous system were significantly reduced or had completely disappeared. We are continuing to learn how the nervous systems of the body are structured and communicate throughout its mass.

This veritable three-pound mass between our ears is considered the most complex system in the known universe, yet the brain is as obstinate as it is complex and fragile. Despite the elegant design of the body, with all its systems operating in symphonic harmony, in a *homeo* or *allostatic* process or perhaps both, the brain has a survival habit of interpreting its environment and, in its discernment, directing the flow of biochemical and quantum-electrical reactions accordingly, thus generating perceptual models of mind, beliefs, thoughts, and memories, which inevitably give rise to behavior, conceptions and imaginings that construct the world in which we live and participate.

By virtue of our very birth, there is indeed a story that is cast or projected outward and onward, as we slip away from the warmth, safety, and unending security of the womb. The protective bliss of an internal, homogeneous zone of automation gives way to an outside world full of chaotic rumblings of all sensorium: a thunderous quake of weirdness. One need only pierce the covers of a thousand books and drift into the gray matter of men's skulls to hear the stories that their births have cast upon them. After all, what is experience but a continuous and distilled flurry of provocation.   Jeff is one such man with whom I had the honor of working.

Jeff would often say to me as we sat together in my office "Who can I tell?" This question was often met with a facial expression, his, that displayed utter confusion, fear, and uncontrollable trembling. After being repeatedly sexually assaulted by a family "friend" almost thirty years earlier, he perpetually reexperienced the event as if it were happening at the very moment during which he spoke those words. He attempted to describe the context in which he felt helpless, boxed in, locked into a frozen, unforgiving environment.

Dad, he said, was a firm disciplinarian from an earlier generation. He didn't show emotion, with the exception of anger and disappointment. "I couldn't do anything right or good enough. How could I ever tell him that our neighbor was, you know...doing what he wanted to me? How could I ever say that one of the older boys at my school was also doing these things?"

In Jeff's immediate, intimate and trusting world, a familiar world of family and school friends, he grew to perceive himself as a helpless waif of sorts. His inner language, his inner view and voice, that personal private dialogue he had within his mind trembled, ridiculed, and diminished the man he was becoming. What was he to do? Where was he to go? The flurry of provocation descended upon him, and his retort was as common and real as breathing is natural, thoughtless, and autonomous.

Like Jason, Jeff's sense of who he was, alas, seemed miles away from the fearful, dreaded and inescapable memories of an innocent youth becoming a confused and rebellious young man- a man who would ultimately turn to alcohol and cocaine to numb the pain of those remembrances. He anesthetized himself in order to deal with his unbearable internal world and the lifelong volley between right and wrong, appropriate and inappropriate. Jeff would say that on many occasions, while taking the city bus to an appointment, a mostly benign event, he would feel quite anxious, fearful, deeply agitated, and ultimately suspicious of older men who were simply, innocently, innocuously sitting alone. For him, these encounters generated flashbacks—disturbing images and memories, rushes of feelings and sensations causing him to literally re-experience the trauma, as if the events were about to occur once again in present day and present time.

As he described it, anger would curl up inside his gut and aggressive feelings would stir as he prepared to defend himself against the ghostly predator; ghostly because the predator of the past somehow overshadowed the innocent man simply sitting on a bus seat by himself. Concentration and clarity of thought were all but lost to a distorted wrinkle in time. The brain does not differentiate between the past and the ever-widening present in circumstances of trauma. That sense of space and distance between what happened long ago that exists as memory and current experience, a simple wisp of neuronal milk, a wisp of neurotransmitter here and a little microvolt of electrical current there, is but a blink of an eye, especially for a trauma survivor like Jeff.

As narratives are sung and intimate histories retold, reflections of the brittle perspective of ignorance in the developing child, Cameron also recalled his dreadful experiences with disdain and a precariously candid appreciation for his own early predicament:

I always had everything I needed.

The problem was the day I met my piece of sh-t father. I was about seven years old and I wish that he would have stayed gone forever. From then on all that I remember is mental, physical and emotional abuse—just every abusive characteristic that you can think of. What I most remember are just a few of the situations in which it happened. The first one being when we went to Maine for a little vacation and I accidentally burnt my Pop-Tart by leaving it in the toaster way too long. I had burnt the counter a little at the hotel and that was definitely not the right thing to do. I can remember the rage that was in his eyes for no real reason. I was barely nine at this time. He was drunk as usual. The anger and complete hatred that bled from his stares were what I saw first as he proceeded to slam me hard. I ran as fast as I could and somehow managed to hide under the desk. When he found me, he dragged me out by my hair as I screamed and kicked as hard as I could.

So enough with that stupid Sh-t because the truth is that even though I was abused, I really can't complain because as I said before, I always had all that I could possibly want or need. So I guess a few good beatings really isn't all that bad...you know. Of course when my brother, sister and I had finally had enough of the good life and started to fight back, was the day that he really decided to take out his anger on my sister. My father got out of work and you could always tell what kind of mood he was in just by looking at him. This was going to be a bad night...I don't remember exactly what my sister did, but when she did it, he went into her room, locked the door behind him and the screams began. His filled the air with such rage. My mother was screaming and crying and tried to get in behind him. She couldn't do a thing. He beat my sister with a metal pipe and threw her radio out the window. My brother and I cried and held each other and screamed.

I think we were ten or eleven when we thought it might be time to start fighting back again. My brother thought it would be a good idea to take a swing at the old man. Not a good idea...Dad beat the living sh-t out of him. He and I ran away that night. The cops found us and brought us back Home even though we said we wouldn't go if he was there. It didn't matter. Soon after that we moved into an apartment and I began high school. My brother ended up going to jail, my sister got pregnant and moved to another city with her boyfriend. I started smoking a lot of pot and drinking real heavy. I started stealing to support my weed habit. Then came the night that my parents caught me drinking and smoking. I don't remember what he did, but I smashed him right in the jaw as hard as I possibly could. That night I left my house and said I would never return if he were still there.

The sad part is, that after all the bastard did, I ended up getting arrested, figure that one out. I spent the night in jail. The next day my mom paid the bail and left my father. I moved back in with her when I knew he was gone. Of course, not too long after that, she would get a boyfriend and move in with him leaving me to take care of myself at fifteen years old. She left me with no money and no means of support. Just gone. At fifteen I was doing pills, heroin, cocaine, drinking and tons of weed. What else did I need? I had everything.

In Cameron's world, in his perceptual kingdom, from the naiveté of his formative years spent in a hostile environment, he indeed had had everything he could hope for. For him, drugs provided safety from unwanted emotional states and means to earn money. He learned to have trust in his own ability to protect himself and see that his rudimentary, immediate needs were met. And yet, even in that fragile space, his *being* somehow had knowledge to the contrary; something was indeed missing, and he longed for that something.

One of the missing and longed-for pieces was foreshadowed by and expressed in Cameron's inability to trust other people and feel close. He would tell me there was always a feeling of being detached or disconnected from others. Traumatic experiences have a way of tearing away the fragile tendons and ligaments that bond people to their families and attach communities together. This is what is termed *depersonalization* in psychiatry. It is as if the events, people, and things were not real but more like a dreamscape or theater production. The translation of the things that were happening was altogether foreign, aloof, and seemingly going on within someone else's life. The pain was perhaps too great to make it his or her own.

Part I

What Constitutes Trauma?

While trauma is always clinically described as a horrifically abnormal event, for any casual student of the human condition, it's actually a perfectly normal feature of history, one that has emotionally scarred billions of men, women, and children since before the beginning of recorded time.

—Mary Sykes Wylie

What does constitute trauma? Trauma is perhaps the most avoided, ignored, belittled, denied, misunderstood and untreated cause of human suffering (Levine and Kline 2007). Today it is becoming common knowledge just how devastating the impact of trauma and the resulting overwhelming sense of helplessness can be to a child's (and an adult's) emotional and physical well-being; cognitive development; and ultimately his or her outward reflections, behavior, and personality development. The understanding of these issues is in large part because of the attention given to the wars in Iraq and Afghanistan and the soldiers returning deformed and re-defined by their experiences.

One can think of trauma as the antithesis of empowerment and yet trauma is so much more than that. It is critical to understand that trauma is not about the event itself or even in the action of the event, although these do of course set the stage for subsequent challenges. Trauma appears to reside in the nervous system, the somatosensory systems of the body itself: the skin, muscle, and other bodily systems. The cells of the body have a large capacity for maintaining very long memories.Trauma is now recognized as a body-based condition, a psycho-physiological event which is very different from a condition based solely in the mind and its thinking machinery (the so-called psychosomatic); however, it is a condition which is driven by both the internal and external environments alike. It is because of this automatic or autonomic triggering of bodily responses that, when a person begins to feel nervous, agitated, or overemotional, and panicky with a quickened heart rate and difficulty breathing, a *panic attack* he or she may not initially understand what's happening. The very physiological response that, in terms of evolutionary function, is meant to give a physical advantage, to help one to survive specific life-threatening circumstances, can become incredibly frightening, grossly detrimental, and profoundly debilitating. The body is reacting to something: *"But I have no idea what happened. I don't know why I feel what I feel. I don't have a reason to feel this way,"* most will say.

Despite being told otherwise and shown evidence to the contrary, many people begin to think that *they* are defective and that *they* are the problem, somehow brought on by their behaviors or how they're thinking. In many ways, the opposite is true. The body's unique physiology is driving the thinking process and is the catalyst for their mental content. Some feel as though they may be experiencing a mental breakdown, not being able to tell what is real, or that there is something uniquely wrong with them, because in their view, *others who have experienced similar situations do not seem to have the same problems and overreactions that they do.*

As we can see in Jeff or Cameron or Jason, that unique physiological process can completely shut down a developing boy and cause great stagnation, bewilderment, and confusion. The intense anxiety and the bubbling or *boiling* physiology within can cause remarkable despair—a frozen, terrorized and powerless state. We cannot simply address the physiological without involving psychological dimensions, mental processes that flow outward from its configuration and determinism.

If we consider that familiar three and a half pounds of neuronal webbing in the human skull called the brain and its prodigious and sometimes disruptive activities, it can be understood to have the basic goal or orientation towards survival: of monitoring and sending out commands to organize and direct – to steer the lobes of the brain and guide towards some behavioral end. Hence, it is sometimes called the organ of survival.

The reptilian brain, consisting of the cerebellum and brainstem and its various components, are the oldest and deepest structures of the brain and are essentially designed and genetically programmed to perceive danger and to activate our fear response system, triggering an extraordinary amount of energy, such as an adrenaline rush or the flow of cortisol stress related hormones, when a predator is bearing down upon us. This release of energy, in the form of a biochemical cascade, in turn increases heart rate and alters many other physiological responses designed to prepare the body to defend itself from the perceived threat. Fight, flight, or freeze are commonly used terms which describe this behavior.

These rapid, involuntary physiological shifts include the redirection of blood flow away from the digestive and skin organs and into the large motor muscles of flight and fight and freezing an immobilization function, along with quickened or shallow respiration. While that shift is occurring, there is also a dramatic decrease in the output of saliva. Pupils dilate to increase the abilities of the eyes to take in light and information within the immediate environment. Blood clotting ability increases, while the ability to speak and other cognitive, executive mental processes decrease in functionality. One need not have a conversation with a lion prior to getting eaten for lunch, as they say.

Muscle fibers become highly excited, often to the point of

tremors in their exerted tension. Alternatively, our muscles may collapse in fear as the body shuts down, becoming completely besieged and overwhelmed with fear. Fight, flight, or freeze are our three basic primal evolutionary survival responses—react to and endure an event. These responses are completely involuntary reactions to life-threatening situations (whether real or imagined) and can be incredibly frightening to the individual experiencing them.

In the case of drug and alcohol dependency, we see that cravings, which can be hailed as the most significant motivating factor for avoiding the sickness of withdrawal, mimic, or may, in fact, be the cause of, these basic and primal physiological changes as the brain concludes that it is indeed being attacked or threatened due to the lack of a particular drug or alcoholic drink. It concludes and responds as if it were in a state of threat and helplessness.

***

Dr. Stephen Porges's *The Polyvagal Theory* (1995) uses the term *neuroception* to describe this automatic and mostly involuntary functioning of our nervous system. Neuroception is the mechanism or sudden synchronization or overlapping of information that triggers neural circuits, regulating the autonomic nervous system (ANS). "Neuroception, distinct from perception, does not require an awareness of things going on", Dr. Porges points out.

This awareness is quite distinct from our own sense of conscious control, reception, and analysis of environmental factors, whether they are internal or perhaps external as well. It is a neural circuit, which could be comprised of hundreds, thousands, or tens of thousands of neurons, and bundles of neurons which are almost *sentient* in their behavior as they evaluate risk in the environment from a variety of cues, such as a loud, unexpected bang, someone shouting at us, or chirping doors. It is not us, but our neural circuits reacting—simply detecting and responding ultimately to the risk or threatening situation. This is why it can be so incredibly frightening when our physiology is so disruptive, and we have no idea what is happening to us.

This purely physiological reaction feels like a panic attack, in fact, it is a panic attack by definition: sudden, rapid, and increased heart rate; sweaty hands or body; an increase in purposeless thought activity; and feelings of confusion, fear and excessive worry. Someone may think he or she is dying or having a heart-related episode. Not an easy experience to endure, as I have many times been told by my own clients.

Although some of the autonomic nervous system's response is briefly described here, it doesn't begin to explore the worm-like characteristics of trauma as it burrows itself deeply into the intrinsic personality, the character traits, social habits, and the underlying neural structures and behavioral patterns that become the lives of those suffering from addictions as they wander in and out of detoxification facilities across the country.

One cannot simply rub up against the flesh of a young man's arm or gaze into his worn face and expect to detect, to become acquainted with, and to identify the deep structural and psychic shifts that have impacted the very essence of his life, his sense of well-being, his personal identity or instinctual drives, his pleasures or dislikes, or his attitudes toward this or that. After all, this sense of well-being and personal identity is partly rooted in the elusive acts, despicable horrors, and worn pathways of emotional thatch and thicket that only he can purport to know. In fact, trauma interferes with forming a well-defined, verbal memory of personal biography, which ultimately results in losing or never attaining a sense of one's *self:* one's personal sense of order and completion or wholeness.

The very content of his mind; his experiential acclaims; his loves; his pleasures and purpose (if ever developed or sought out); and his talents and imaginings, both developing and untapped, are brutally, despicably beaten down, prevented from emerging, and held like prisoners of war, although without a visible guard or gatekeeper. His self-expression and self-awareness is like a bubble of air trapped beneath a tumultuous flowing river of life. Memories, all the bits and pieces of experience, neither taking root nor shape show no buildup of a personal essence.

***

During our everyday experience we casually toss around words like my*self, me,* or *I,* but *w*hat does this really mean? What is it? Where does it reside, and how does it grow, if it grows at all…this *self, me, or I*? Is this ownership, this spurious subjectivity, an emergence or a predetermined set of charges from which to elaborate or necessitate some evolution? Is it merely a means or an interface through which and by which to interact with the world?

V. S. Ramachandran, MD, PhD, the director of the Center for Brain and Cognition and professor of psychology and neuroscience at the University of California, San Diego, describes aspects of the self in his attempt to delineate us from other species in his beautiful book, *The Tell-Tale Brain.* He suggests that there are seven fundamental aspects through which the self is broadly characterized:

1. The sense of unity: Feeling like we are actually one person; with all of our goals, memories, emotions, actions, beliefs, and present awareness we form a coherent, single individual.

2. Continuity: Despite the enormous number of distinct events punctuating our lives, we feel a sense of continuity across time—moment to moment, decade to decade. Continuity imposes a sense of lineage.

3. Embodiment: We feel anchored and at home in our body. Trauma has an insidious way of grossly disrupting this aspect of self. Consider the story of Jason and his brother whose single-twin identity was at times fractured,

constructing and consisting of multiple parts. Embodiment also includes our body image. This is my arm, my leg, etc. Dr. Ramachandran states that, "it never occurs to us that the hand that is holding our car keys might not be ours", (unless of course there has been a medical malfunction of brain circuitry from stroke or other forms of trauma, causing a disruption called *anosognosia*).

Although this is a rare condition, there are people who, upon suffering a stroke or some other unfortunate medical trauma, lose the internal mapping machinery or neuronal connectivity that would typically include such information about their body parts: internal, intuitive knowledge that this is *my* arm or *my* leg. These are *my* hands and feet. When I scratch here, the itch is upon *my* brow. In fact, people with this very peculiar condition will in some cases choose to have their alien limb, the one that just happens to be there, amputated altogether, thus making their bodies feel whole and theirs.

4. Privacy: We come to believe that our mental life belongs solely to us. Others are unable to penetrate the boundary of our inner life directly.

5. Social Embedding: This quality of self maintains a sense of privacy and autonomy despite its reliance on others within our community. It's interesting that almost all of our emotions make sense only in relation to other people: pride, arrogance, vanity, ambition, love, fear, mercy, jealousy, anger, hubris, humility, pity, and even self-pity. There seems to be a persistent drive to be connected to and part of something.

6. Free will: We also have a sense of being able to consciously choose between alternative courses of action with the full knowledge that we could have chosen otherwise. This is, of course, a subject of much debate, as replicated studies demonstrate that the brain and its circuitry are activated or processing milliseconds, and even seconds, before we are consciously aware of choosing an action, suggesting that our brains are choosing before we show up

to take credit for the conclusion.

7. Self-awareness: This is an interesting aspect, as it implies an awareness of one's enduring point of reference, but it really arises in the context of being aware that someone else is aware of you.

It is perhaps, at the very least, about an organization of the contents of mind   centered on the organism that produces and motivates those contents and the bio-emotional glue that binds it.

Although it might be humorous to think that there may be a little conductor inside the brain, commonly referred to as homunculus, who stands with baton in hand, waving and ecstatically stirring about saying, "Here...now there," with various information and imagery, we know that this is not the case. There is however an orchestration, a mysterious synchrony of information that somehow gives rise to or is generating this conceptual framework known as *self*.

As I write about this notion of trauma and its tragic side effect—addiction, and this idea of self, I cannot help but think of one's disposition—his or her set of developed responses and methods for managing life's events and doings. It seems to me that this disposition is the central grouping of core beliefs and understandings or rules of how and why things are the way they are—why things happen or are, perhaps, prevented from happening. Armed with all those whys, wherefores, and hows, some subconscious order is established and an identity is born. A complexity of seemingly random and chaotic happenings becomes unified. Conceivably, we can call this the self, myself, yourself, me or I.

Perhaps another way to bring this rather vague and elusive concept of self into our understanding is to think of it the way that the neurologist Antonio Damasio does in his very dense and elaborate book on consciousness, *Self Comes to Mind*. He likes to think of the rich complexity as one having a mind equipped with an owner, a protagonist for one's existence, an inner witness inspecting the world inside and around, or an agent seemingly ready for action.

***

In attempting to describe what trauma is, it has been suggested that it becomes stratified by degree of intensity, duration, and frequency of occurrence of trauma inducing events, making the interpretation of trauma a complex and highly subjective discernment. What may constitute trauma or come to be a trauma for one individual may not necessarily be experienced as such by another. The inner witness or personal authorship housed within the confines of the human mind generates something very singular and enigmatic: a perpetual and robust assimilation of experience.

Many studies involving twins have demonstrated this effect of uniqueness and interpretation. The translation of a significant event or even a series of prolonged stress provoking events into a hardened neural network, pattern, or fixed way of perceiving and interacting with one's environment is a vastly subjective, phenomenological one, the ownership of which belongs to the individual alone. It relies not only upon one's historical and autobiographical information, but also the remembering, reordering, and infusion of that history in combination with the relevant emotional arousal attached to it, essentially providing the meaning of the experience itself. What does it mean that my mother has died or my uncle seduced me? What is my place, my position, my disposition in this meaning, as part of the overall transactional process.

And what about this strange idea of remembering or reconstructing, as if one were piecing together that which had been lost or forgotten or broken up? For that matter, what is memory and how does it come about at all? Recall that one of V. S. Ramachandran's seven aspects of the self is privacy; we come to believe that our mental lives belong solely to ourselves. Others are unable to penetrate the boundary of our inner lives directly. That inner life to which he refers is the memory of and the details of the events and experiences of our lives.

In brief I have always considered memory to be comparable to a mental file cabinet, one in which was stored and filed away the vast accumulation of data encountered from day to day. In fact I used to think, as was standard paradigm, that memory, *my* memory, was held in some very specific, private place in my brain, a dedicated clump of cells that, when pressed in some fashion, would somehow magically spill out its contents, revealing all that was being sought.

Today, neuroscientists believe that memory is in fact far more complex and subtle than that. It seems that memory is located not in one particular place in the brain, but is instead a brain-wide or global process, which includes the participation of any number of brain systems at any given moment of necessity. For example, the memory of how to operate a bike comes from one area that is actually made up of a vast quantity of data and draws from many regions across the brain. The memory of how to get from here to the end of the block comes from another, again with an enormous collection of data located in many areas in the brain. The memory of biking safety rules comes from another, and that nervous feeling when a car veers dangerously close comes from still another.

Each element of a memory (sights, sounds, words, emotions) is encoded in the same part of the brain that originally created that fragment (visual cortex, motor cortex, language area, etc.), and recall of a memory reactivates the neural patterns generated during the original encoding within that same region.

The latest findings from neuroscience suggest that a more appropriate way to imagine our memory system might be as a complex web, in which the threads symbolize the various elements of a memory, which join at intersections to form a whole, rounded reminiscence of a person, object, or event. Neurologists are only beginning to understand how the parts are reassembled into a coherent whole.

Eric R. Kandel, MD is a professor at Columbia University, the director of the Fred Kavli Institute for Brain Sciences, and a senior investigator at the Howard Hughes Medical Institute. Professor Kandel's research has been concerned with the molecular mechanisms of memory storage in Aplysia (a large sea slug) and mice. Through Dr. Kandel's research, we now understand that memory and learning, for that matter, are processes and changes that happen at the synaptic level of the neuron. Synapses are strengthened or weakened by assorted factors which enhance or cause to decay those reminiscences.

I have, of course, simplified the rather dynamic and fluid process we call memory here. The fact is that memory is perhaps a misleading term, suggesting the storage of something. In some cases it does appear that individual cells do have memory—a system of encoding, storing, and recalling information, which they can access without the help or input of multiple brain areas. Facial recognition, for example, in some people has been shown by a single cell. By and large however, it appears now that the process of memory, the process of gathering input from many entry points throughout the body's sensory systems, co-creates a network of data that, when stimulated by an event, sound, or other means (which I will discuss later), produces a reasonable facsimile of information deemed useful for survival. In trauma, this information can be released in a very frightening way, as I mentioned earlier within the context of fight-or-flight responses of the autonomic nervous system (ANS) or a complete and total freeze response, as directed also by the ANS.

So what does make an event indeed a traumatic experience? How does that neural webbing pack such a powerful and enduring punch, which lasts sometimes an entire lifetime? No one escapes without some form of stress in this life, it is said. Stressors pervade our every waking moment and often our dreams, too, yet there is considerable tolerance of extreme situations. As of yet there is no measurable understanding of the subtle conversion of an event into a complexity of fear and survival responses that can terrify an individual into paralysis and plague life's journey.

Just as water has its boiling point, emotionally significant events thrown into the path of a developing child also reach a point of no return, that point at which the nervous system instinctively takes sending out commands to the body to take a defensive action. "Protect the organism!" it expresses. Neuroception, the decision making neural circuit event that evaluates risk in the environment from a variety of cues, underscores our awareness and allows those primitive nervous system responses to take over, thus inhibiting conscious and deliberate executive choice and action. Such special characteristics and unique conditions must be present in order for the trauma to be a trauma.

***

Vast amounts of information are contained in the moments, the exotic and the mundane, which make up the instances of our lives. Seconds, minutes, hours, days, months and years, all variety of the instances which are captured like that of photos at the hand of a skilled photographer make up the variety of our moments. Our senses are percolating with the information embedded in each instant of experience. Many Trillions of bits of data flow with ease into the dynamic matrix of the brain, giving rise to a seamless sense of continuity and internal unity.

We tend to take our senses for granted, assuming they will always be there to absorb the outside world, deconstruct it, and piece it all back together into a coherent whole from which we can live our lives successfully and unscathed. And yet we continue to learn about the many shared brain structures and neural networks giving rise to a seemingly continuous experience no matter how piecemeal and disorganized it may appear in its initial staging. It's simply amazing to think that my experiences, ideas, thoughts, feelings, likes and dislikes, creative endeavors, intimate relationships, and cravings may be thought of as a collage, comprised of tiny bits of something, almost holographic in its primordial nature. But here I am—here we are—in full form with prodigious acclaim.

I think most people are familiar with a form of painting called pointillism. Perhaps you're familiar with the famous Degas painting *Sunday in the Park* for example. Tiny dots of color applied to a canvas many times over eventually display a unified and comprehensive picture of beautiful park dwellers for all to admire. The image becomes meaningful only when the millions of points or dots appear to become connected as seen from a distance throughout the canvas, creating a work of art upon which to gaze. Each of our moments are casual and without value as they stand alone, but through the context of our aliveness, meaning is established.

***

We live primarily in a visual-spatial world, a world of sight. An assemblage of photons is drawn into the brain through our eyes; it then morphs into color, shape, intimate details of line and thickness, the brightness of daylight, or the darkness of night. Sight grants us depth through binocular vision, movement and form matched and synchronous. Each color is coded by its shading and the intensity of contrast. Photons of various light spectrums wander, dropping into the eye and settling upon the retina with its multitude of rods and cones (sensitive to different color spectrums), where they make their way into deep structures within the brain's visual cortex, the occipital lobe, through the triggering or excitation of a variety of cellular mechanisms, groups of nuclei, a dance, perhaps of bio-electrical magnetism and quantum fluxuations.

The electrochemical pulses then inevitably *choose*, through stimulation, various cortical pathways called the "old pathway" and the "new pathway," terms referring to the evolution of brain structures within the discipline of neuroscience. They then split off again into the "how" and "what" pathways. There may even be a new pathway call the "what about" pathway, helping to give rise to a consistent picture of *what is*, separately analyzing and coming together to cause the perception of unity, indeed a perception or percept in all of three-dimensional space in which to create and act with purpose despite the fact that there are physical, structural gaps in the anatomical machinery which gives us the perception of unity.

How does what we see impact the fabric of our selves, from the perspective of the traumatized person? The process, the activity of sight generates a language through which to communicate an experience derived from what we have seen. It creates a field or snapshot of those elements present at any given time, which come to dance in the retinal field of vision and within the brain structures which then interpret the dance or interactions of people, places and objects.

As we know, people, places, and objects of varying importance take on a rare significance, perhaps a reluctant importance, during times of trauma. The substance which our vision has captured—for example, where someone was standing or who they were standing with suddenly becomes an internal cue: a significant bit of information remembered and used repeatedly to trigger the nervous system which causes one to respond to the threat. What style clothing was being worn; was it bright, cheery, and colorful or dull? Was it new or tattered clothing? What was once fleetingly banal, mundane—relatively insignificant and superficial, just an everyday occurrence, not too important or noteworthy— suddenly becomes stubbornly fixed in the brain. It becomes burned into the cavity of the enduring self, setting one up to be sensitive to subtle cues from the environment which appear similar in nature the sensory cues during the event itself. It's branding lodged as if our memory was a rawhide and that tragic experience a searing hot iron being mightily heaved into the flesh by some invisible, muscular arm. This is trauma!

Historically, according to V. S. Ramachandran, vision may have evolved primarily to discover objects and to defeat camouflage. He's referring to the idea that things are often hidden from our view and in many ways hidden from our perceptual view as well.

Imagine, he suggests, your primate ancestors scurrying up a tree trying to detect a lion seen behind fluttering green foliage. What you get inside your eyeball on the retina is just a mass of yellow lion fragments obscured by all the leaves. But the visual system of the brain "knows" that the likelihood of all those different yellow fragments being exactly the same yellow simply by chance is zero. They must all belong to one object. It links them together, decides it's a lion and sends a big "a-ha" signal to the limbic system-emotional system (reptilian brain), telling you to run.

Within our attention—our subjective field of experience—vision builds a bridge of significant detail, meaning that there is a distinction between what is and what is not important to pay attention to: what may be harmful versus what is safe. From that detail a memory is coalesced to draw conclusions generating a future projection or anticipated effects, actions, etc. Sight gives to us a representation of occupancy and our other senses complete the scenery for a full tapestry, a vast three- or four-dimensional context of experience. In the end, sight offers to the brain, to the mind, and to the self a method of evaluation, an evaluation of environmental substance. This is the collective visual substance of trauma.

***

Like sight, the accumulated effects of smell and taste also burrow deeply into structures of the brain as they capture chemical molecules hidden in the air—hidden at least from our conscious, alert, and perceiving mind. Perhaps a fire was lit and a smoky perfume filled the air with its dense, unyielding, and pleasurable fragrance. Perchance particular perfumes or that very distinct bodily odor which we are able to perceive between people has become ever present within us as to never forget it.

The olfactory bulb structure is one of the oldest and most fundamental structures to ensure our evolutionary survival. The olfactory bulb transmits smell information from the nose to the brain's limbic or emotional system, bypassing the need for conscious evaluation. Although that system can become corrupted, it plays a critical role in emotion, memory, and learning.

In keeping with what constitutes trauma, let us think about a rape or incest victim. There may have been alcohol or additional substances involved, which become engrained in the sensory system. The taste or simply the smell of beer or wine may be enough to trigger a reaction. Was the smell a sweet one or possibly one of a hideous odor? The unique signature of a smell, such as ammonia, bleach, a fragrant flower, or burned flesh, can be captured by its pungency or sweetness laying out the perceptual (our awareness) and the neuroceptual (our nervous system's awareness) path to facilitate remarkable and unwanted changes to the nervous system.

***

What was the temperature like during the unfortunate events? Was it cold or warm? Did humidity fill the room or space being occupied at the time? What was the season: winter, spring, summer, or fall? Imaginably the victim was shivering or sweating or thirsty. All sensory data coming in, a litany of it filling the brain with involuntary information about the external environment, gets recorded, seized by our anatomy, encapsulated, and utilized by the billions of specialized nerve cells that make up the brain and nervous systems to make predictions about future similar situations with similar sensory environmental factors.

To make this information a little more accessible and concrete, let us consider a man named Rock. Rock was a sixty-two-year-old Vietnam veteran who entered the military at eighteen years of age and experienced more trauma than most of us will hopefully ever experience in our lifetimes. Rock was a *grunt*, a foot soldier in the jungles of Vietnam and therefore endured long days and nights and a full range of seasonal climate changes as he hunted for the enemy in an effort to survive and carry out his mission. As we might imagine, the sensory data that invaded his brain was utterly relentless and included a variety of temperatures, barometric pressure changes, and changes in humidity levels together with all other senses being overrun and flooded with information. This is survival! In this environment the conscious mind is set to autopilot while the neurons and cells that make up the nervous system call the shots. Remember the concept of neuroception, in which the neurons act through their own volition.

Rock and I would have long talks about his experiences and what I learned from him was that the most powerful sensory stimulus or trigger that he recognized was that of temperature, the warmth and humidity of the jungle atmosphere. As spring and summer came around, Rock would instinctively, unconsciously, impulsively, and without planning sabotage anything good that was happening in his life at that time and move himself into the woods where he would live, survive, feel at home and feel safe. Sensory cues —neuroception, caused an internal flood of biochemistry and physiology that overwhelmed Rock's ability to function from day to day within society, which he experienced as hostile and threatening.

Anxiety, irritability, flashbacks, panic attacks, exaggerated startle response, hypersensitivity, hyperreactivity, and avoidance behaviors, all of which are the common dissociative symptoms of post-traumatic stress disorder (PTSD), now called post-deployment syndrome (PDS), were borne out during the spring and summer months. A state of hyperarousal, during which the sympathetic nervous system keeps the body on red alert, controlled Rock's inner life and hence his outer behavior. Rock's sympathetic nervous system was in full swing, fully aroused, essentially shutting down executive function and bringing to the fore all primitive and reptilian functions leftover from an earlier evolutionary existence. In fact, most of his life after the Vietnam War was spent living in the woods, isolated, sheltered, protected—physiologically responding to a fear of something that no longer existed in real time but did very much so in brain time, meaning that history was being relived day after day. The brain was not living in the present moment but as if the past traumatic events were repeatedly happening. This is the corruption of the *now*. This is what trauma can do.

***

Rock had become a hunter of nothing in the middle of nowhere. Paradoxically, sorrowfully, it was his own interior, his relentless physiology that was the actual hunter/protector/prosecutor. Rock attempted to elude himself, his inescapable sense of urgency, fear, and rumination, which tormented his waking life. This was where he was most comfortable. One might be tempted to suggest that this was where he was directed to go by the very nervous system and deep brain structures that kept him from perishing in the jungles of Vietnam almost thirty years earlier. This is the survival response. This is an example of how the nervous system, a biological system created for survival, can lead to an organism's slow destruction and ultimate demise.

Interestingly, we are not aware of the thousands, tens of thousands, or trillions of bits of sensory data that actually impress upon our physical bodies as we move through our days or sleep through our nights. In fact, it has been hypothesized by numerous neuroscientists that we may be less than 1 percent conscious of any such processes, and therefore, our concept of choice or free will is nearly nonexistent—although it would please the author if it were the other way around. However, if we were aware and of conscious control of all this data we would cease to function. This is the genius and built-in protection program of creation and evolution. During times of trauma, it can easily be stated that this program becomes part of one's awareness and we can see the results clearly enough through Rock's reality.

We have a propensity to react only to those stimuli that are loud enough, strong enough, or developed enough in their presence to warrant an action, some sort of output or a behavior. Although the tightening of our muscles, especially in our necks and backs, are common, even these procedural responses are done mostly outside of our awareness. How many times per day does one clench his or her teeth or tighten his or her jaw? These are mere reflexes that do not require one's presence of mind (for one need not be there). Given enough time, however, and as the pain increases, the individual's threshold for pain tolerance is reached, and he or she may consciously choose to relax those muscles that had been stimulated subconsciously or perhaps see a chiropractor or masseuse for relief.

As with the senses of sight and smell, we experience an incredible host of sounds from day to day, most of which go completely unnoticed. Depending upon our living conditions, natural or man made, synthetic sounds may force their way into our ears and onto our cochlea and then make their way into relevant structures in the brain for interpretation. Birds and tractors, the scream of a child, the siren of an emergency vehicle, or perhaps the gentle laughter of lovers inevitably become absorbed and screened within the brain's vast neuronal networking machinery. How many sounds don't we hear? How many sounds never make it to our awareness for conscious transmission and evaluation? Consider the subtle hum of a ceiling fan or a broom drearily sweeping.

Now imagine the footsteps of a doting parent and the meaning or narrative that slowly develops: the memory of being tucked in or being read a nighttime story. Quiet anticipation gives way to giggles and to a wondrous joy and connection as the footsteps get closer and louder, and the door opens to the sight of a trusted parent. Excitement builds in the moment and spills out with laughter amid the warm feelings of safety and belonging and trust.

The emotional boundaries are being laid down and established like a labyrinth of roadways and fences connecting distant cities and townships. Now imagine that those same footsteps were the very sound you heard right before a perpetrator opened your bedroom door to render you helpless, crying in pain, and frozen in a state of terror. Associations are drawn, characterized, and concluded in very different ways. Hearing, like all other senses, establishes a context of sounds—mere vibrations—and makes them important by circumstance and meaning. Emotional values are assigned and distributed.

The sounds of footsteps meant suffering, anguish and torment to this child, like Jason and his brother, in his telling of "Noises, lights and sights" at the beginning of this book. As he and I would sit together, the normal, everyday sounds like doors closing, a light switching on, those steps of my colleagues or his peers coming down the hall, or a book falling onto a desk would cause endless jolts and ceaseless twitching throughout Jason's body in a helpless and powerless state of anticipation of horror.

***

Like the aforementioned senses of sight, smell, and sound, we cannot discount the sense of touch as a source of stimulation and a precursor of memory, either, as it is needed in virtually every action we undertake. It may be the most overlooked sense and yet every one of us receives tactile information about the world around us every second of the day. How we choose to hold something or stroke our hands against an object provides our brain with direct feedback as to its position, telling a story of safety or danger. Gripping a baseball during a game is defined by the intention to participate with the game itself.

The grip, the tightening of the fingers and the deliberate release all within a specific context characterize the meaning and the emotional value, the abstraction of the touch experience. The sensation of touch never goes away except of course with age and some neurological disorders. Even then, we still sense the squishiness of our buttocks as we sit in a chair. Touch is unique, says David Linden, a neurobiologist at Johns Hopkins and the author of *Touch: The Science of Hand, Heart, and Mind.* Linden points out that you can close your eyes and imagine what it might be like to be blind or block your ears and imagine being deaf, but touch is so central and ever present in our lives that we can't imagine losing it.

We feel the cool breeze of summer lightly brush against our faces. Finding a bug crawling on one's forehead causes a brief reaction—maybe a fleeting bout of panic. The sense of touch is inexorable. The hair that lightly hangs over our shoulder and tightness of our shoes are among the many touch sensations that bombard the skin, our second-largest organ, the brain being the first, at every moment. What information does the skin offer? How about the feel of a paper cut on the tip of your middle finger or the discomfort of a speck of debris in your eye?

According to Dr. Linden, there are two main systems of touch. The first system organizes facts, location, movement, and the strength of a touch. The other is an emotional system of touch. This emotional system of touch deals with social bonding, the sensation we get from a hug or even sexual touching. There is a significant slowdown of processing of information in these bonding touches. It may be easy here to understand why it can be so difficult for the survivor of a sexual trauma, a violation of the most intrusive kind, to learn to trust the touch of someone, even someone whom they might have been with for some time.

***

Trapped within the skull, the brain has no direct experience of the external world as mentioned previously.

It is hidden and protected. The brain relies on the outward reaching senses to teach and guide it toward safety and survival. Neuroscience and neuropsychology inform us that the brain generates symbolic descriptions, representations of objects and events in the external world, having no actual experience of its own. These maps arise in the form of nerve impulses, which have a very intricate and complex language of their own, the code of which will need to be cracked in order to understand the brain more completely in years to come. For now however, we know that any given object or event will evoke a potential unique, brain-wide patterns of activity, propelling chemicals, and electrical currents around the brain. Such patterns of activity represent visual objects in much the same way that squiggles of ink spread out on paper represent a description of your living room in the form of a letter or word. The brain considers input and creates a representation of what the external environment might—and that's a big might—be like, so that the body can emerge in safety and exist with limited risk and harm.

***

Imagine…says "E"

It all started when I was four. I was taken away from my parents who were also addicts. My father wouldn't stop beating on my mom. I remained, trying to help but I was just too young, too small. My father would take me and roll me up in a rug and push me aside. The state finally got involved and I was placed in foster care. I'll never forget that judge. Soon after, I was placed in the custody of my grandfather.

Life was good for a while. Then on my twelfth birthday my mother came back into my life. She got custody of me once again and I moved back in with her. Not a good idea.

My mom had a series of nervous breakdowns and ended up hospitalized many times for being suicidal. She continued to use drugs so that all of our money, what little we ever had, went to buy them. We had no hot water and the fridge was always empty. I remember taking freezing cold showers and eating breadcrumbs, never mind the verbal abuse. I finally had enough. I'll never forget the time I walked into Shaw's Supermarket with an empty backpack scared to death. I said a prayer and went for it. I filled the pack and walked out the door. We never went hungry again. They would follow me around the store as they started to catch on so I'd change my routine. I don't know how but I never got caught. God must have been protecting me. I never felt good about it. .

When I was fourteen I met my friend who turned me on to selling weed. We were both dirt poor kids growing up in the projects. I hated rich kids and where we lived they were all around our little community of poor people. I began to learn the ways of the street. I began to rob those kids and their families so that I could pay the bills. Eventually I got caught and got on probation.

I would spend a lot of time in state custody from that point on. I learned how to fight and earn respect for myself. When I finally "aged out," I ended up back on the streets and started getting into weed again, because it helped me to not feel any feelings. I then got into cocaine and booze. Me and my friend began selling cocaine and living like rock stars; partying all the time. We did everything together. We were becoming big time dealers and acting like kings. DEA began following us and we just kept on doing it all. At one point we were supposed to make a pick up and I had a bad feeling about it. I chose not to go and it was a good thing because it was a set-up. The cops got my friend and his stuff plus all the money...over a hundred grand. I didn't get caught but I had half a kilo at my house and no way to pay for it. The dealer wasn't happy. I spent three months watching my back wherever I went.

One day I came home and my house was lit up like Fenway Park. The dealer had placed a pipe bomb on my front stairs. When you pick it up it should have blown me up. My mother picked it up but it didn't detonate because it was apparently one volt off. The bomb squad blew it up. ATF harassed me for many months after that. I then got real humble. I got a job and tried to do the right thing. Then my grandfather died and I couldn't deal with the pain. I got into Percocet's and fell in love with them. Eventually I moved to Oxy's. I moved to dope, and got arrested.

***

Our family, friends, classmates, and the other social communities that we become involved with and endeared to are all rich with potential sources and provocations of trauma. In addition to what "E" has written, his sharing was rich with other horrific details. For example, he was given up for adoption because his biological parents would repeatedly burn his tender one-and-a-half-year-old skin with a lit cigarette. He found himself with foster parents who seemed to care and act in a loving way initially.

It would not be long, however, until his foster father would begin sexually molesting "E" when he was four. His foster mother found out eventually, divorced this monster, and soon began dating other men. These other men would commit violent acts toward the foster mother. "E" responded by attacking these men in defense of his mother to little avail. A ten-year-old boy is no match for a thirty-year-old, two-hundred-pound drunk, unstable, and unpredictable man.

Trauma grows like a virus and is sustained by repetition, although a onetime event can certainly be sufficient to generate an enduring imprint as well, and should not be underestimated. Take Bruce, for example, and his powerful memory of a tragic childhood event. One which left its mark very deeply and painfully.

"Bruce" went to his best friend's house when he was ten years of age. When he arrived, his friend wasn't home, but he found an ominous note on the door that read "Do not come in…call 911." Bruce ran home terrified, viscerally sensing that something was wrong, and obediently called 911, as the note had directed him to do. Later, as he watched the paramedics pull his friend's father out of the house, he looked toward the unzipped body bag as it lay atop the rolling gurney and reluctantly peered in. As he did, the horror consumed his fragile boundaries and the safety of what he had thought was good, predictable, and stable up to that point in his early development. He saw that the posterior of the head of his friend's father had been completely blown off. It was indescribable and unknowable in its horrific and grotesque state. Sometimes one event is more than enough to endure.

The sight of that at once penetrating thing that lay haplessly zipped in a black bag once was a friend's father, someone knowable, with warmth and existence. Now it was a frightening and lifeless corpse that offered no explanation, no understanding, and no identity. What did this mean now? How was Bruce supposed to make sense of this? What story could be told about what had happened? One event was enough to start the flowing river of trauma for this innocent child.

***

Like all of the tragic and possibly heroic stories which inform the traumas detailed here, "K" a young man bearing the hallmark of traumas cruelty revealed to me that one day, he had taken some friends to the top of a high hill and provided drugs, other substances, and paraphernalia to have a party, an innocent and fun party. A time of celebration and happiness. As the day turned into night, and the people present became intoxicated and grossly impaired in their judgment and ability to walk, one of the kids, an eighteen year old boy, lost his balance, falling to his death.

Never-to-be-forgotten, random acts suddenly turn bad and trauma is born in that instant, shattering constructed boundaries of safety and understanding. It is carried forward with enduring prowess and dynamic emotional pressure from within.

"K" was unable to forgive himself, unable to dissolve the image and knowledge of his young friend's death. As he continued to blame himself, bearing full responsibility, "K" spiraled into addiction with no way out. Heroin numbed his pain and buried the emotional weight he carried, and tragically his body would soon be found by strangers in a nearby park, partially decomposed perhaps metaphorically much like the internal representation which he had constructed of himself: unworthy, unwanted, and lost.

The Role of Boundaries

Neurologist Dr. Robert Scaer describes a patient whose boundaries had indeed been shattered:

Jane came into my office clearly in a state of distraction and fear. She had been involved in a relatively low-speed auto accident two months before, and instead of improving, she had begun to experience worsening cognitive and emotional symptoms. She has begun to misplace things constantly, had spells of severe physical weakness, had fallen several times, and had developed a stutter. At other times she felt agitated and fearful, and was intolerant of any stimulus, including noises, bright lights, and even simple conversation with family and friends. Even brief exposure to these seemingly minor stimuli produced confusion, anxiety, and ultimately exhaustion. When I examined her, she visibly jumped, and then pulled her arms tightly around herself when I walked around the back of the exam table to examine her spine. When asked, she stated that she felt extremely anxious and uncomfortable when I stood behind her out of her field of vision, even with a female chaperone in the room. Her past social history revealed that she had experienced a physically traumatic rape at age sixteen. She acknowledged that she had always been uncomfortable when she was in a crowd with people behind her whom she could not see. In a classroom, a theatre, or at a party, she usually positioned herself with her back to the wall.

What exactly are boundaries and how does the individual, from birth through early development and well into adulthood, develop them...construct and design them to meet individual needs?   In many ways boundaries metaphorically resemble the fences and walls neighbors place between houses or plots of land to identify borders and points of demarcation. Boundaries are emotional and physical separation zones that identify what is ours, mine, and theirs. They imply ownership and possession. They offer a qualifier for *somebodiness, a* personal identity, one deserving of safety and security.   Within these zones is the stuff of recognition and freedom to be expressive in a way that satisfies and creates happiness while supporting healthy risk taking.

We all live in a small and safe world of our own, defined by invisible but very real perceptual barriers or boundaries. These boundaries are formed by our collective experiences within the world around us. Some of these experiences are positive and rewarding, some negative and possibly punishing. Associations of pain or physical or emotional discomfort or the withdrawal of rewards become linked to the negative experiences better known as conditioning. Perhaps one of the earliest pains we experience for example is the disapproving frown of our mother or father even in infancy. The parental response produces shame and creates the first boundary in the perception of that unique bond. All of our senses—smell, taste, vision, hearing, nocioception (sense of pain), proprioception, (sense of motion), and touch— contribute to the formation of these boundaries, these perceptual and emotional zones of belonging. They tell us where we end and the rest of the world begins. We are grossly unaware of these perceptions that allow us to move about in the world without literally impacting obstacles that are not part of our own selves.

As developing infants and children, we receive positive and negative information from sensory experiences that contribute to our perceptions of safe boundaries. For example, I could think to myself, in an automated, unconscious way, "This is a safe place with these safe people to express my likes or dislikes. I know that I will surely be accepted and not ridiculed or beaten up if I do." Painful or unpleasant feedback leads us to avoid moving beyond the boundary created by that experience, whereas positive feedback stimulates us to explore the area within that boundary, taking healthy risks where the opportunities to learn can move us into a new rewarding and exciting career path or allow us to make new friends.

These sensory feedback loops continuously help inform and redefine or rebuild our boundaries, inviting us or intimidating (inhibiting) us. We develop a very specific internalized map or pattern (*patternicity*, an idea I'll refer to later in the book) of how we can safely challenge or be engaged with the world around us. The more stable and solid our boundaries, the more safe, secure, and effective we will be in dealing with both the world outside of ourselves and the world inside ourselves; we create our own very personal and enduring point of reference. We've all seen the shy kid or the excitable, overzealous child in the playground. Which one do you suppose has the confidence to be self-expressed? Our boundaries forge an internal pact: the courage to walk toward others or the fear that keeps us away from them.

***

So how do these invisible boundaries inform or relate to trauma? Remember that we form boundaries from feedback received from those who nurture us from the very beginning of our lives. Hopefully and with a little luck, our sense of safety is such that we are able to form strong attachments to the people who surround us and build up a powerful protective space around ourselves. This helps to guide and generate an internal sense of warmth, trust, comfort, and safety, affording us the ability to expand into a larger boundary space: i.e., to push the boundaries. These early experiences shape the boundaries in our young, developing lives and are temporal, as they shift throughout our lives, allowing for perceptions to change, new relationships to form, and an internal sense of wonder to spring forth.

In safe, trusting, and loving environments, our caregivers are always there to address the hurt, discharge the threats, and help us to understand and rebuild boundaries that become ruptured through negative experiences, cultivating optimism and hopefulness once again. A strong sense of self and those protective boundaries separating us from the rest of the world give rise to a resilience with which to deal with hostile situations. However, in threatening environments such as the one described to me by a former client, "P" in which his mother, addicted to crack cocaine, would perpetually come into his room and assault him physically, beginning when he was about eight years old, those boundaries become grossly distorted. The sense of a safe separation between himself and the rest of the world was shattered in those very fragile moments. The safe havens of his body and his room were ruptured and the boundaries closed in and shrank leaving him in an unsafe, suspicious and apathetic place.

Eventually, as "P" got older, he began to protect himself by placing heavy objects on the top of his door, which he'd leave open a crack. When his mother came in to abuse him, she would be struck by the object, giving "P" the time he needed to get to a safe zone to protect himself, if for but a short while.

Indeed, one's very existence is perhaps based upon his or her perceptual boundaries. Therefore, even the threat of harm to a caregiver with whom a child has developed a sense of safety and relationship can potentially represent a threat to his or her own existence as well. Consider Michael's story:

When I was fourteen years old, my mother was diagnosed with breast cancer and eventually did die. I was prepared for that, though. When my brother died two years ago, I couldn't see it coming. It was a shock. I had no preparation, no good-bye time, and no way to say I love you and I'll miss you.

As Michael continued to speak he told me something I

was not expecting:

"That's not all", he said casually. *"These were two big events in my life, but when I was ten years old, my best friend was lured into a stranger's car, suffocated, sexually assaulted, stuffed into a plastic box that had been weighted down with a concrete bag, and dumped into a river."*

The horror of that knowledge for Michael was unforgiving. This is something which he had no internal capacity to manage. He was helpless in his youth and experience to cope with such tragedy. This is trauma which is not a personal physical attack but rather one which occurs within ones very special, safe and familiar boundaries called secondary trauma.

Secondary trauma is trauma that one may be exposed to by the news media or family or friends who suffer a horror such as Michael's friend, and it can leave a track of insurmountable pain and psychic discord that lingers long in the body and the mind. This form of trauma is as insulting to the individual as if the trauma had happened to him or her. The intensity and the brutality are branded nonetheless, embedded in his or her cells, casting long shadows upon his or her memory circuits.

As our boundaries become distorted with the onslaught of these childhood infringements, our intrinsic sense of self, our inherent safe haven becomes a continuous threat. As a child approaches adulthood, everyday tension and threat that might be considered trivial by many people, tend to be seen by the child as representing the difference between remaining alive and being in fear for their very lives. The child loses their resiliency; the ability to bounce back; gone are willingness to test the world and push the boundaries of creative exploration and involvement with others for the purpose of growth, change, and exploration typically considered healthy risk taking behavior.

Imagine being the youngest of seven children and considered the black sheep of the family. Fred's mother would make him sleep in the chicken coop rather than with his siblings. When she was really upset, she would make their family dog have anal intercourse with Fred while his siblings watched to teach them a lesson and give a stern warning and example of what could happen if they disobeyed her.

When Fred was an infant, his mother would put alcohol in his bottle to keep him from crying and get him to sleep. She would also leave Fred and his siblings alone, as she prostituted herself with a variety of men. Fred's boundaries were overrun, indeed shattered, as he became dependent upon alcohol, and chronically homeless, living alone like Rock in the woods. The difference however, was that Rock was pulled by his physiological distortions of time and compelled to live alone due to a perceived threat which no longer existed in real-time, whereas Fred's sense of worth and personal value had crumbled leaving him alone and destitute.

Corby, too, is an example of what happens when that unique psycho-dimensional safety zone is ripped away or not permitted to grow and develop in what would be considered a well-adjusted and healthy way. Corby was a twenty-six-year-old man with four children of his own, but he had no custody rights and lived alone. At the age of seven, Corby had been shot up with heroin by his parents. He had also been sexually and physically abused until he was about nine years old. At that time, Corby's brother took initiative, and they both ran away from home, but got entangled in the foster care system—a system of child management often with many disturbing outcomes of its own. Corby was subsequently abused in many of the homes that were expected to be protecting, guiding and nurturing to him.

Like so many of these men without the ability or the internal structuring to be able to form the consistency of a stable and original identity—what we call someone's personality—Corby developed borderline personality disorder (BPD). He attempted suicide multiple times, generally as a means of self-affirmation, and engaged in self-mutilating behaviors often assumed to be used as an attempt to gain attention. There was no sense of an absolute, ever-enduring point of view or a self within Corby. That self, comprised essentially of the personality traits of others that he unconsciously adopted as his own, was a fabrication of others' experiences and perceptual conclusions. None belonged to him alone; he had no historical or individualized personhood or ownership. His self was the *self* of others.

Boundaries are a delicate fabric forming a womb of trust through emersion around an identity seeking direction into an unknown world. Here, rather than the building up of attachment and inclusion, there is a cruel erosion of the simple beginnings of what should be the quilt of safety in which one is warmly held. Deep emotional memories are constantly churning in the deepest regions of the brain, the limbic system, and one's global associations determining one's behaviors, attitudes, thoughts, and perceptions for a lifetime and forming a physiological prison from which there may be no escape.

I Thought It Was Normal

I know that most men, including those at ease with problems of the greatest complexity, can seldom accept even the simplest and most obvious truth if it be such as would oblige them to admit the falsity of conclusions which they have delighted in explaining to colleagues, which they have proudly taught to others, and which they have woven, thread by thread, into the fabric of their lives.

—Leo Tolstoy

Many young men as well as older men do not identify the many tragic and violating events in their lives as traumatic in the sense that we are referring to them here. Many men consider these events to be normal occurrences, as matters of fact and routine, and as regular, customary, or usual habits in their own lives as well as part of the lives of others.

Luis told me: "My father was a preacher, he preached in the church and to us, his kids, at home…at the dinner table, in the park…anywhere. He constantly extolled the virtues of being American and after the attacks of September the eleventh, 2001, my father would forever say that "they're coming for you too, son. They're gonna draft you to fight. You had better watch out for yourself."

Imagine hearing this rhetoric day after day, spoken with passion, as if matter-of-fact. The conviction as real and probable as the eventual morning sun rising upon the horizon.

Perhaps if one were well-equipped as a developing and naive child, one might wonder if the rhetoric was true or even possible and consider questioning its veracity, its authenticity, and the likelihood of its coming to fruition.

We grow up within the confines of circumstance. We're born to our parents, in their place, and there are no choices there. Theirs are the faces we see most often, or perhaps those of our aunts, uncles, or elder siblings. It remains their faces to which we become attached, beholden, guests in their home. Everything connected to those faces, that collective countenance of early living, belongs to us and no one else; it is our sovereignty—part of our developing boundary systems. It is proprietary in nature and selectively ours to possess or by which to be possessed, directed, and led.

As infants, we suckle and are dependent upon our caretakers to get all of our needs met: from feeding to elimination, from protection against the elements to a safe and hospitable sleeping environment. We depend upon their generosity of spirit and their acquired wisdom to guide our fragile and developing bodies and the selves that lie tucked away for some future awakening or broadening and expansion.

***

There is an old adage that says a fish cannot tell that it is wet until it is removed from the water. When we grow up in environments in which the norms include violent disagreement, anger, physical rage and threat, hopelessness, negative expectations, dreadful criticisms, and failure, then those attributes and traits become the expectations, interactions, and normal patterns of living.

These patterns may have existed for two, three, or four generations without resolution, without change in the lives of many young men, becoming their lifestyles, and unfortunate inheritances. Perhaps these behavioral codes began with their great-grandmothers, were learned and adopted by their grandfathers, and then passed on to their fathers or mothers. Men learn how to move away from people by withdrawing, hiding themselves, and keeping secrets from others. There becomes an inescapable and expectant world view that says simply, "This is what I am, and this is how I do me."

This idea falls in line with the gross development of belief systems. A belief is maintained by "knowing" that what it refers to is most likely true, beyond questioning, and will remain an absolute. Beliefs of great proportion have been responsible for many tragic events throughout history such as the rise of Nazi Germany or the Spanish Inquisition. Consider our example of the fish in water. It's always wet. It came to exist within this state, having nothing to compare. Likewise, we routinely trust what is presented as a fixed reality, the honesty of which is not in question.

Like Luis and the account of his father's preaching and the fish that can't know what wet is until it is suddenly without water, young men are born into a very private world that thunders with the telling of parental character, traits, and pedagogy, as they are cast down—a self stuck in time. Many truths are given and go unchallenged. Take this example of John, who sat in my office as we spoke about why he was crying uncontrollably. Tears were flowing as he sat quivering in sadness and obviously hurting to a great extent.

When asked about what he was feeling, John casually replied, "I have no idea what I feel. I don't feel anything." He could not authentically describe what feelings he was experiencing at that moment with me. He had no way of identifying the physiological or emotional state that was dominating him, crushing down upon him. It was as if he didn't actually experience or maintain an association with the very feelings or emotions that controlled his behavior for these moments we were together. He had no language with which to identify and describe the stuff of his suffering. As we sat and talked, it became quite clear that because of how his father had reacted to his expressions of sadness, disappointment, hurt, loneliness, fear, confusion, or the like, John had learned to repress and disregard these emotional states, but his body—the physical experiencing of those states—couldn't be so easily manipulated. By virtue of the magnitude of suffering by so many lost men, it is obvious that our somatosensory systems record all, whether we know it and can recognize it or not. Our mental activities may not have maps of understanding or comprehension, but the body is fully awake to all experience.

***

Earlier I mentioned the concept of *patternicity* when talking about the role of boundaries in one's development. In his book *The Believing Brain*, Michael Shermer wrote, "Imagine that you are a hominid walking along the Savanna of an African valley three million years ago. You hear a rustle in the grass. Is it just the wind or is it a dangerous predator? Your answer could mean life or death."

Our brains are belief-generating engines, evolved pattern-recognition machines that connect the dots and create meaning out of the patterns that we think we see or we do observe. In the above example, if the hominid hears the rustle in the grass and, more often than not, finds that there is indeed a dangerous predator awaiting his arrival, then his brain will connect these two dots or events to form a pattern in order to protect and preserve the life of the Hominid through association. It's much like tracing a maze with a pen until you identify the exit.

Likewise, many men are taught that it is simply not OK for a man to cry and express his feelings. He is shown by painful example, facial expressions of loathing, disappointment, or perhaps a slap across the mouth. "*I'll give you something to cry about*" is sadly a fairly common response by many fathers and, as has been written previously, by many mothers as well, to the simple cries and requests for guidance by an innocent child who seeks direction and nurturing. When all that the child truly desires is to be held and gently coaxed into the right behavior, a sense of placement, and comprehension, he is instead made to feel like damaged goods, defective hardware, made wrong by ignorance and the courageous act of being humble against an unforgiving world of shame.

This is the pattern: (A) The child demonstrates fear or confusion or perhaps cries for direction and is met with (B) a slap across the mouth or a derisive look, representing the meaning, "I'm wrong or I've done something bad or perhaps I'm worthless and no good and broken." The child is scorned and shamed. The brain naturally looks for and finds patterns and then infuses those patterns with connotations of value, forming stories and beliefs. Beliefs become his methods and motives, his backbone, and, generally speaking, his very reason and impetus—perhaps providing the initiating impulse for interacting with his world. In a very primal way, this ultimately renders the emerging personality that the child comes to identify as himself.

Recall the seven fundamental aspects of the self as modeled by V. S. Ramachandran at the beginning of the book. One of these is being one's own enduring point of reference.

George shared the following with me

My mother would always bring home these Lebanese men while my father was at work. I was five years old. Imagine that I'm a five-year-old kid and these men would give me candy and chocolates to keep me quiet. "Shhhh," they would say, "don't tell your father." My mother would nod, agree and say "this is between us." Then my father would come home and I'd be stuck between having this knowledge, these memories of these strange men coming into my home to be with my mother and not knowing what to do with it. I loved my father, I still do and I still haven't told him almost twenty years later. I love my mother too, but I knew it wasn't right. I'm still stuck between loyalty and the pain of knowing. I hate her...it was, is torturous. Imagine my own mother. What kind of mother would do that to her son?

The often unanswerable questions, including the one that George asks, represent the impossible despair and loneliness of its inquiry. They are in many ways the secret yearnings that burrow themselves in the deep and silent utterings which habitually haunt the psyche, commanding its collapse and conciliation.

Neuroscience and evolutionary biology continue to reveal new information about the brain and its multifaceted and wondrous capacities. It has amazing abilities to adapt to circumstance, both perceived and actual, because it doesn't know the difference between the two in all cases, as we have seen. Its dynamic and rich structures self-organize feedback loops, which are responsible for providing necessary data to all of the systems available to it: the nervous systems, the circulatory system, the endocrine system, the somatosensory system, and many, many more. Patterns become conditioned, and a reality is forged.

The normalization of dysfunctional family patterns manifest and nurture an unhealthy learning environment. Within this environment, social skills of adult living are malformed, underdeveloped to standards far below the norm. This results in a grossly inaccurate and naive perceptual sense of reality; a distorted view of life. This becomes a developmental state of atrophy and the genesis of emotional blindness, stunted intellectual growth, and a perversion of precise feeling and sentiment. This is the pattern for many men as they endure such dehumanizing and agonizing environs. A signature of trauma. A maladaptive soup of emotional discord.

Part II
What Is Addiction?

Now that we have heard from many men through their stories about the unfortunate and tragic patterns of their young lives, which were born out of horrific and desperate circumstances, let us look at the most prevalent way they are acted out, adapted to, and sustained: through the onslaught of the prodigious and indiscriminate process called addiction.

In many ways addiction has become the new trauma or certainly the continuing escalation of the precipitating trauma as it guides men's decisions, leading them into the most desperate, perilous, and threatening lifestyles imaginable. These hideous and dangerous lifestyles are in stark contrast to a healthy, productive, and meaningful life. Phantoms in the brain run amok, perpetuating the same type of feedback loop as when those emotional boundaries were shattered earlier in life, leaving a helpless waif in the destructive path of a relentless tide of uncertainty. His primal instincts fulfill their roles in fostering a fight, flight, or freeze response, a biological salvation.

Drug addiction has remained a stubborn, evocative, and insidious problem for individuals, families, and societies for thousands of years. It is only in the past twenty years or so that science has been able to clarify one of the factors: addictions cause lasting changes in the human brain that are difficult to reverse, according to an article in the *Journal of the National Library of Addictions* (May 2011), summing up the unfortunate departure from a balanced and flexible brain.

Although we have new insights into the flexibility or plasticity of the normal adult human brain, the brain hijacked by addiction becomes wired up, programmed in limiting, inflexible ways over time. It seems that only the drug of choice, as it is commonly called, can satisfy the cravings and need that appear as powerful as the threat to survival itself. Addiction can be likened to the necessity of breathing for one who is beholden to it. To be without their drug is to not take a breath. The floundering about, the emotional and physical gasping for it is unequivocal in its havoc, which erupts from moment to moment, day to day.

Thus the current working definition of addiction as stated by the National Institute on Drug Abuse (NIDA): *Addiction is a chronic, relapsing brain disorder in which the addict /alcoholic has lost control of his or her ability to choose whether to take or not take the drug in the face of negative health, social, or legal consequences*. Moreover, addiction in the broadest use of the term, is as morally neutral as it is reprehensible. It makes no choice between the banker and the mother as to who will become its next victim. Can you imagine that, as a result of ingestion of narcotics, you overdose and slip into a coma, not once but twice, or maybe even three times? You are in an unconscious state for days or weeks. When you awaken from the coma, without thought or continuity of critical reason, regardless of the fact that your family is with you and your doctors inform you of the risks, you immediately discharge yourself from the hospital (after all, you are an adult) and desperately run right back to the street, to your dealer for another fix. You simply *must* have the drug! Incidentally, we haven't even discussed the cognitive impact of being in a coma or the acute (immediate) and long-term effects of cerebral hypoxia, a brain deprived of oxygen, which compounds the challenges of choice.

Addiction's indiscriminate methods of choosing its victims adds to its insidious nature: the way it meanders through the relationships and casual conversations between and among friends, family, or professionals like lawyers, police, and teachers. Innocent curiosity and attraction can lead to total devastation, as beautifully portrayed in this aptly titled, anonymous, but well-known poem about addiction:

I Am Your Disease

You know who I am, you've called me your friend

Wishes of misery and heartache I send

I want only to see that you're brought to your knees

I'm the devil inside you, I am your disease.

I'll invade all your thoughts, I'll take hostage your soul

I'll become your new master, in total control

I'll maim your emotions, I'll run the whole game

Till your entire existence is crippled with shame

When you call me I come, sometimes in disguise

Quite often I'll take you by total surprise

But take you I will, and just as you've feared

I'll want only to hurt you, with no mercy spared

If you have your own family, I'll see it's destroyed

I'll steal every pleasure in life you've enjoyed

I'll not only hurt you, I'll kill if I please

I'm your worst living nightmare, I am your disease

I bring self-destruction, but still you can't tell

I'll sweep you through heaven, then drop you in hell

I'll chase you forever, wherever you go

And then when I catch you, you won't even know

I'll sometimes lay silent, just waiting to strike

What's yours becomes mine, cuz I take what I like

I'll take all you own and I won't care who sees

I'm your constant companion...I am your disease

If you have any honor, I'll strip it away

You'll lose all your hope and forget how to pray

I'll leave you in darkness, while blindly you stare

I'll reduce you to nothing, and won't even care

So, don't take for granted my powers sublime

I'll bend and I'll break you, time after time

I'll crumble your world with the greatest of ease

I'm that madman inside you...I am your disease

But today I'm real angry...you want to know why?

I let all in recovery, entirely slip by

The Boy in the Chicken Coop

How did I lose you? Where did I go wrong?

One minute I had you…then next you were gone

You just can't dismiss all the good times we've shared

When you were alone…wasn't it I who appeared?

When you sold those possessions you knew you would
need me

Wasn't I the first one who stepped in and agreed

Now look at you bastards, you're all thinking clear

You escaped with your lives when you found your way
here

Only fools think they're winners when admitting defeat

It's what you must say when you're claiming that seat

Go ahead and surrender, if that's what you choose

But, I'm not giving up, cuz I can't stand to lose

So stand in your groups and support hand in hand

Better choices will save you…leaving me to be damned

Well, be damned all you people seeking treatment each
week

Be damned inner strength, however unique

Be damned all your sayings, be damned your clichés

59

Be damned every addict, who back to me strays

 For I know it will happen, I've seen it before

Those who love misery will crawl back for more

So take comfort in knowing, I'm waiting right here

But next time around, you'd just better beware

You think that you're stronger or smarter this time'

There isn't a mountain or hill you can't climb

Well if that's what you're thinkin', you ain't learned a thing

I'll still knock you silly if you step back in my ring

But you say you've surrendered, so what can I do?

It's so sad in a way, I had big plans for you

Creating your nightmare for me was a dream

I'm sure gonna miss you...we made quite a team

 So please don't forget me, I won't forget you

I'll stand by your side watching all that you do

I'm ready and waiting, so call if you please

I won't let you forget me...I am your disease.

The willful and innate tendency of both body (somatic) and mind (cognitive/behavioral) to maintain a cultivated and enriched system of operation--patternicity is sung here concisely. The poem both ridicules and accentuates the ill-fated, maladaptive, and continuing reward functions of the brain, whose calibrations are exquisitely tuned and yet sometimes malfunction, to our detriment.

This pattern of malfunction is similar to the autonomic nervous system's (ANS) response to a perceived threat, not an actual threat based in the here and now; an actual problem to be resolved. Remember that the ANS acts through neuroception, or cell consciousness, making its own choices through procedural memory and directing the production of neurochemistry such as Adrenaline, Cortisol, and, Norepinephrine the function of which is to activate the body to ensure its survival.

Often, the addicted person will state, "I don't know what happened. I was doing everything right, and now here I am, trying to figure out what the hell I did wrong." With today's advances in neuroscience and technology, specifically functional magnetic resonance (fMRI), a clear distinction can be drawn between the organic activities of the brain and the expression and communication activities of one's mind.

In fact, it is a valid statement when one says "I don't know what happened." During the course of a relapse, a return to active addiction, there is a dissociation or disconnection that occurs during the triggering process, in which cravings prevail over conscious judgment and willpower. The objective over the subjective. Many of the brain's reward systems are acting at the level of the neuron in the anterior cingulate cortex, in conjunction with other deep brain structures that are known to be involved in regulating emotion and personality, such as the orbital frontal cortex and, eventually, the ventral striatum.

What is telling here is that the part of the brain that is used for reasoning and decision making, called the dorsolateral prefrontal cortex, is quiet at these times, as if offline or inactive—essentially muted and asleep. There is evidence through neuroimaging that there is a clear separation between what one knows (what one is conscious of) and what one's brain is experiencing and thus responding to.

There is a story about a young woman whose basal ganglia—a very unique midbrain structure that helps to control head movement, eye winking, limb movements, etc.—suddenly and shockingly began to misfire. One day, her head began spontaneously turning to the left. She experienced no pain, no cramping, nothing that appeared to be an obvious physical change. After some time, her head began not only to turn to the left but also to snap back as if held by a rubber band whose tension suddenly released. Her eyebrows, too, then began to move up and down involuntarily.

As all this was occurring, she lost control of her mouth, her tongue, and her cheeks. In desperation the young woman began sending mental messages to herself in an effort to gain control, but to no avail. Later, she discovered that she in fact had had an allergic reaction to a medication that she had taken earlier that day. The medication was meant to control nausea but instead attacked her vital basal ganglia, causing a loss of control over her body: in effect, separating her mind, her conscious *will*, and deliberate effort from her brain, much like the addicted person's unfortunate experience. Her brain had been hijacked by a drug as well. Those behaviors were completely out of control.

***

It should be no surprise, then, when we talk about addiction we reference it as being an entity of its own. As the above poem says, "*I am your disease*" and those who are addicted and have become dependent will say, "it wasn't me. That's not me!" when confronted with the horrors of desperate behavior. Addiction dominates and attacks those in its path like a flu pandemic: families, places of employment, significant others. As the addiction grows and the addict becomes desperate for money with which to cop (street slang meaning to purchase his or her drug of choice), all those mentioned within their sphere are suitable targets from whom to steal and plead for forgiveness for a second, third, or fourth chance. Said one young man mournfully, "In five weeks I lost my house, my car, my job, and my kids."

I recall one other young man who would, upon experiencing the unfortunate pains and pulls of withdrawal from heroin (described as flu-like symptoms but much worse, including restless legs, cold and hot flashing, runny nose, and repetitive picking at the skin, usually the face), threaten to stab or slice his own throat as his first method of manipulation to get what he wanted, which was always money. When this failed him, he would then proceed to literally throw himself down the basement stairs in front of his family. This of course would inflict great pain, which made the man even more enraged and desperate. I have known young men who have called the police on themselves, planning to engage the police in a shoot-out as a sad attempt to have the police take their lives and end their misery, a phenomenon known as "suicide by cop."

***

Those with addiction face numerous other obstacles beyond brain chemistry and their basic physiology, however. They often underestimate how challenging it is to stay clean, to live on a day-to-day basis without relying on their substances of choice, especially during their first attempts to remain abstinent, known as early recovery.

Many men have alienated their peer and family support systems along the way, and having burned these bridges, have few places left to turn. As a result, many of our men continue to expose themselves to dangerously unhealthy environments, friends, and acquaintances, who may be enabling their old ways, inviting them back, seducing them with the drugs they seek so badly. One seventeen-year-old man told me that, because he was homeless, he lived with his elderly dealer. In exchange for sexual favors, he was able to remain off the street, be provided with shelter, and be cared for. The shame and guilt of this behavior, this desperation, held him a prisoner to his dependency. To own this history of deprivation and recklessness is often cause for great despair.

It's not uncommon for men to have multiple relapses in their efforts to remain drug free. The willpower, the sheer force and command that it takes for one to avoid the people, places, and even objects, media etc., that remain a synchronous part of everyday life for the addict or alcoholic are unimaginable to those of us without such proclivities, such helplessness, and such vulnerability.

For a moment simply try to envision oneself unable to read, to understand and interpret the squiggly lines on this page. The challenge is epic and life-altering when success is at hand. In an ironic twist, it is precisely at the point of success that one is most vulnerable, most susceptible to relapse. For many of these sickened, beaten-down men, there is indeed a great fear of living life in a meaningful, productive, deserving and loving manner, especially when it comes to self-forgiveness—the terrifying act of loving and accepting oneself in the face of all that has gone before. The lying, stealing, and manipulating to secure drugs, not to mention violent or illegal acts such as home invasions, armed robbery, even assault and counterfeiting are parcels of addiction.

A report from Columbia University's National Center on Addiction and Substance Abuse (CASA) portrays just how challenging it is to break the bonds of addiction. If someone begins his or her journey into drug or alcohol dependency after the age of twenty-one, he or she has a one-in-twenty-five chance of remaining addicted for life. Those whose addiction's start before the age of eighteen fare even worse. They have a staggering one-in-four chance of developing a a lifelong dependency. The statistics don't lie; if anything, they may not reveal the ugly truth that the numbers are most likely minimizing the reality of who is actually out there, struggling to stay alive even as I write this line. Indeed, the numbers are high and unknowable.

The Abyss of *Non*-being

The subtitle of this book concludes with the phrase "*And the addictions that sweep them away,*" which is a direct reference to the mindless abyss of *non*-being, to which these addicted, often traumatized men succumb. There is a sense of time standing still or having stopped and suddenly restarted, as the addicted person awakens from his or her chemical coma. It is often said that an individual remains fixed at, or relatively unchanged from, the developmental age at which he or she began to abuse illicit substances. There are as many possible reasons for this to be so.

Despite the lack of congenital or developmental problems, which could lead to any number of cognitive-behavioral pathologies, many of the men whom I meet with, do in fact, appear to be stuck at very early ages, perhaps around the twelve- to fourteen-year-old level, just around puberty, which is marked by massive hormonal upheavals and developmental crossroads.

Many of these men have had little education—generally, through seventh or eighth grade—were diagnosed with attention deficit disorder in early childhood, and come from single-parent homes, where stress levels were not necessarily well-managed and healthy coping strategies were lacking. It is as if many of these men have literally ceased being able to learn, not from a lack of intelligence but rather from the inability to apply newly acquired knowledge or to progress beyond the very adolescent mannerisms and patterns of thinking that tend to broadly epitomize that time in a young person's life.

Peer pressure is pervasive, individual vocabulary is dull and basic, the use of language itself seems rough and still incubating in its development. The ability or desire to forecast and project themselves into a future state is sorely inadequate. Instead of an expansion of self, there seems to be a persistent inhibition and withdrawal.

When thinking of language, one rarely considers the dynamism of the intellectual complexities that lay in wait for an explosion of curiosities and questions. In fact, as Oliver Sacks points out in his exceptional book *Seeing Voices,* "dialogue launches language." Language launches the mind, and once it is launched, we develop a new power, "inner speech," which is indispensable for our further development, our very thinking. Lev Vygotsky also writes (and informs much of Sacks's writing) that indeed we *are* our language, but our real language lies in inner speech, that ceaseless stream and generation of meaning that constitutes the individual mind. One of the top thinkers in the field of addiction medicine, Terence Gorski, calls addiction and this state of *non*-being a "progressive personality disorganization."

Interests and hobbies are characteristics that would be associated with a teenage cohort. Iterations of the adult are stifled and the expansion into this new developmental realm do appear as though they have fallen short of what one would expect during graduated developments. The young person's perceptual capacities reflect less than average introspection. Self-awareness is somewhat dry and shallow. Motivation and attitudinal shifts vary, but what is lacking are the material and substantive qualities that go along with intentional and purposeful activities. Their individuality is overshadowed by an immaturity, a juvenile irresponsibility, and a deafening of adolescent wonder and curiosity.

This is of course not the case for all, but by and large has been prevalent among this population. Many men will actually state, "I feel like I'm still a teenager" (despite being thirty-nine years of age, or perhaps fifty-four). "I don't know how to act like a grown up, cope, and live independently. I don't know how to pay bills or be responsible or hold down a job or maintain a bank account. I've never done it before."

Using a slang phrase for beginning to use drugs (typically heroin or other opiates), they will say "I picked up when I was ten or twelve, and I was off. I have never known any other way to live."

I talk about these individuals as men, but the more accurate description would truly be boys. These boys certainly have become encapsulated within a stereotyped stage of development. Within this period, this journey to nowhere, they are enriched only by the hunt for their preferred substance. The moment of completion and fulfillment comes as the hunt ends. The drugs are found, purchased, and consumed. Soon after, there is another completion and fulfillment period, as the drugs are ingested and registered in the brain's reward system.

The reward is short-lived. Upon undertaking an assessment of past choices and activities (assuming the capacity for being mindful exists), Individuals often become withdrawn, anxious, and terribly disappointed in themselves. Guilt, shame, and self-loathing often give way to continued "using" as a means of self-medicating. Flattening, or dulling and numbing the individual to any emotional experience, is nonetheless the new inhibiting factor, perhaps overshadowing the original traumatic experience, but certainly adding to its canopy of pain. This is known as avoidance behavior. One cannot look at or allow oneself to experience the emotions which are currently manifesting or those emotions that have been locked away or stuffed down for so long.

***

Being stuck within adolescence also tends to leave many of these men socially clumsy and unable to acquire new meaningful relationships. In many ways isolation becomes the rule rather than the exception in daily life. Generally, these men keep a variety of the same friendships that were developed during elementary school, which tend to be of similar persuasion and proclivity, but even they are often ignored during periods of active addiction. Other relationships come about in the form of occasional connections and become a means to an end only: items to be collected and quickly discarded when used up.

These associations lack emotional and personal attachment of any kind, no long term commitment to another's well-being. They merely serve to provide transient company and are completely understood in this way. The basic need lies in acquiring the drug of choice and succumbing to its dictates. Aside from the rare romantic relationship, the acquaintances have little expectation of one another. The newness, freshness, and exploration of a new and meaningful relationship with someone is avoided or simply not possible within the self-limiting actions of addiction and the everlasting hunt. Most, but certainly not all, relationships which happen within active addiction are of a superficial nature.

This does not mean, however, that these men are emotionally bereft or without conscience or that the potential to develop solid, mutually rewarding relationships has inevitably dried up and passed them by. It merely speaks to the challenges that lay ahead as these men have literally been left behind and must now begin to nurture skills that most people their age have already mastered.

Many men are aware that they're lagging behind and will often speak, with remorse and melancholy, of what they lost or have never been able to accomplish or achieve. They readily compare themselves to others—their old friends, coworkers, and family members—with a sense of envy, desperation, and hunger to have what those others have.

They perceive themselves as if they were a void, an incompleteness, or something that has yet to begin.

Opportunities have passed them by: the girl, the job, and the material possessions that help create a stable and enduring sense of self. Belonging, and grounding have all but washed over them as they watched, as if from a state of paralysis and immobility, stuck and ridged and awkward.

***

Memories that others may speak of with pride, connection, personal reflection, and ownership are all but lost on these men, these boys. The experiences that serve to generate an historical, deeply personal, and autobiographical identity often are blurred and smeared out across vast stretches of time and bear no resemblance to a life having been lived or participated in at all. I suppose in many ways this life can be compared to that of someone who has suffered some unfortunate medical trauma like a stroke, a brain injury, or a dementia of some kind and surfaced with a retrograde amnesia. There may be no tangible bond to a past. So, in a manner of speaking, these men have lived in *absentia*, alienated not only from others but also, measurably and qualitatively, from themselves.

Consider this moving remembrance from "J":

When I was ten years old, my father first injected me with cocaine and by thirteen I was injecting heroin. My father became my running partner and my mom used also. I ended up in a bunch of foster homes where I was abused both physically and sexually. I then went on to get incarcerated for petty stuff: shoplifting, writing bad checks. Hell I'm twenty-two now and just figuring out how to trust somebody, anybody, let alone try to figure out what's good for me.

Many times I have heard men say, "Please tell me what to think, how to think, because I don't trust my own thoughts. They got me where I am…I don't trust them…Would you?"

Listen to the particularly poignant words of Mat, whose

story accentuates the misery, loneliness, and despair that is essentially that abyss of *non*-being:

I started at nine years old being put on Ritalin and then Seroquel and Clonidine because they said I was hyper. I hated it and I when I didn't have it I tried suicide. Then a couple of years later my uncle, dad and grandma all died. Then I started to drink every other day and then every day with the Clonidine. I started getting into cocaine and crack. Then my papa died and I didn't say nothing. My friends were dropping out [dying from overdosing] and one went to jail for life. I felt lonely, I feel lonely and then I became homeless. I started to be on the streets, being drunk on the road taking suboxone and sleeping in hallways and shelters. I kept trying to get into detox but was red-flagged [meaning that, due to previous behaviors, he was not eligible for services]. I can't take it no more. If I don't get into a halfway house I'll probably do something so I go to prison for life too or I'll slit my wrist.

The sad, do-or-die, and appalling reality here specifically for Mat is that he may never regain or recapture a sense of aptitude beyond that of the ten-year-old little boy who resides within him. Such a cry for help may never be heard. He will develop skills as an adult perhaps (he is nineteen years old), but such skills will be limited to brute and brawn, possibly and most likely, without the emergence of a dynamic and richly cultivated mind. The physiological damage, the cellular destruction, the lack of family support, and the many other distressing biological and sociological factors will most likely act upon him in ways that, for now at least, are unpredictable. For him, the youthfulness and innocence of a childhood will be forever lost in the shadows of addiction.

Part III

Addiction Knows No Bounds

Despite their cries of despair and their often degraded and humiliating manner of survival, these men do somehow stay alive, albeit along a slender thread. They demonstrate a resiliency that is uncanny and unexpected. Is it the human spirit, the innate optimism, an evolutionary impulse to survive? Or is it sheer luck that has afforded them this continued life despite their awkward refugee status, that of an outcast, as is often the case with the chronically homeless, addicts, and alcoholics?

Partially as a consequence of their traumatic history, partially as a residual side effect of desperation, and partially due to other extraneous factors, these men have ironically developed skills to defend against and survive experiences that many of us would not survive in similar circumstances: sleeping outside during the harsh, cold, winter months; foraging for food in garbage cans or dumpsters; and sleeping in them, too: their willpower, their drive, their capacity to survive is amazing. As another example of survival adaptation: when incarcerated, these men accustom themselves to the personalities of their fellow inmates, and the culture inside. Many men have developed the perceptual skills that put their heads in the right part of town, meaning that they have learned street rules and possess a keen intuition about territory, jargon, and street markings.

"Imagine that you are a hominid walking along the Savanna of an African valley three million years ago. You hear a rustle in the grass. Is it just the wind or is it a dangerous predator? Your answer could mean life or death."

In many ways the perceptual and instinctual skills and proficiency which I have witnessed are no less than one would expect to see in a young, developing child as he or she attempts to get his or her immediate needs met through ongoing parental neglect. The acting out, the manipulations and half-truths, however deceitful, do tend to elicit favorable responses. Daily needs, whether met by stealing, shoplifting, forgery, dealing drugs, aggression, or robbery, do tend to be fulfilled—at least to a degree. One's morality, one's values, and one's civil humanity are set aside—although this is often a subtle, slow, and unconscious process. Modesty, vanity, and other characteristics of an introspective and comfortable life also vanish alongside the addiction process.

***

From bankers to barbers, it is true that addiction has no bias, no preference, and no prejudice toward race, sex, religious expression, socioeconomic class, profession, or upbringing. In fact, I have had the great pleasure to have met addicts who were brilliant mathematicians (published), firemen whose lungs have been burned and scarred, writers, and inventors alike.

I have spoken here mostly of men to whom addiction has brought abject and uncompromised misery. Addiction can be less harmful but still a heavy burden to bear for some who are less obvious and more inconspicuous, such as the banker to whom we hand our money for deposit, the pharmacist who prepares and hands us the much-needed prescription written earlier by the doctor who may be himself addicted to the very prescriptions he pens, the high school English teacher who teaches our children and does so with integrity, the loving grandmother who walks her grandchildren to school every day while their parents are at work, or the priest who preaches the gospel on Sunday to help shape and guide the religiously oriented.

It's easy for a simple prescription, perhaps a much needed script for pain relief to morph into a full-blown addiction in a short span of time. I currently meet with many people, men and women of all ages from diverse backgrounds, who became dependent after having had some medical procedure performed, often in their teenage years, and may times after surgical childbirth. I routinely have people tell me, "I had my left kidney removed and my doctor gave me a prescription for Percocet. I said, 'No I don't want those; I don't need them.' But he just handed me a script anyway. I couldn't say no." My clients then go on to say that their doctors would simply continue to fill the prescription, sometimes for years, never knowing that their patients were addicted, never following up or educating them in any meaningful way. The current medical climate has changed offering much needed appreciation for addiction prevention somewhat, as regulations for monitoring narcotics and other habit-forming medications have tightened and limitations have been placed on how many times prescriptions for certain medications can be filled and to whom they can be given. However, I still hear about conversations between my clients and their doctors: "You're going to need them. Take them." Often this is done without information on the habit-forming nature of the drugs. This can also be said about dentists, as I have routinely been told.

Medications for anxiety are also often handed out without regard for consequences. There is a specific class of medication called benzodiazepines. These, like opiates and opioids [synthetic form of opiates], are highly addictive, and have been abused and over-prescribed. Many people arrive to see me, stating that they have been prescribed a particular medication for the past ten years or more, without any review of its therapeutic efficacy. These folks are addicted and some don't even realize it until they run out and begin to have bizarre dreams and behavior, such as hallucinations or worse, perhaps a psychosis with violent acting out. When the nervous system causes the heart rate to increase, produces sweaty or cold sensations, and becomes easily overwhelmed, the patients may have a panic attack and /or feel like they are dying. This, of course, is due the nervous system's setting off a false alarm, perceiving a threat where there is none. Drug withdrawal is dangerous business. And with alcohol and benzodiazepines, withdrawal can actually lead to death.

Addiction knows no bounds, has no conscience, expresses apathy at every turn, and is as unforgiving and relentless as a mudslide, an avalanche, or a cancer. There are no known instant cures for addiction. For some, the process is a lengthy and slow-moving progression of dependency, beginning in the teenage years as fun, explorative dabbling, and experimenting, while others are immediately seduced, transfixed, and hooked into its dreadful promise of euphoria and a pleasurable numbing of emotional pain. The end result, however, is the same: a total collapse of identity, social isolation, and emotional instability. Hence, a life has been sacrificed, given up, and snuffed out. It's time to rebuild.

Good-bye Letters and Poems

Life changes sometimes gradually and oftentimes quickly.

We often refer to addiction as being in a relationship, albeit a curious one. It's a relationship because of the intimate connection the addict forms with his or her drug(s) of choice. It is no less a relationship than that between two people who spend time together, plan activities, and feel the myriad emotional states that pervade its grip: the experience of satisfaction, bitterness, ecstatic pleasure, and resentfulness.

A relationship with addiction is a very tangible because there is indeed a bond that may be nearly inescapable due to the pain one would likely endure if one were to end such an attachment. There is a longing that accompanies the hunt for the drug and gratification when the hunt is resolved. It may seem odd or peculiar to envisage addiction in this manner, but as men are beholden to the ones they love, they are equally beholden (or more so) and under the spell of the alluring and intoxicating substances to which they run, or often crawl, in disgrace and suffering.

Often the men I served would write good-bye letters and poems to that drug as a symbolic gesture toward ending this often-fatal relationship. I've included some of their letters here with permission. They reflect the prodigious vulnerability of the authors and the insidious manipulation of these substances as addictions sweep in and take over the lives of these men.

The Boy in the Chicken Coop

Randy writes:

This letter has been a long time coming and we both knew it. In the beginning it had been fun ya know, weekend bonfires after football games. Then after we graduated and were legal (remember the eighteen-year-old drinking age) we started seeing each other more. Playing softball for the tavern didn't help. Sure I saw others once in a while, but you were always my love and you and I both knew it. For a long time we kept it pretty casual two or three times a week and most weekends. Then in 1986 I got married and the other woman in my life joined in the fun (although never as much as I). She was one of those weirdo's who could drink and stop. But you and I had a very special love affair. You were there at all the most memorable moments of my life. My friends and family loved you as much as I did and some loved you more than me. My wedding day, anniversaries, birthdays, shit let's face it you were with me almost every day. Sure I never saw you before work, but as soon as work for the day was through, you and I would take up where we left off the day before. We had an understanding; you'd allow me to hold a job and even thrive at it and I in turn made money so we could continue our love affair. We never suffered any legal problems and so it went day by day, week by week, month by month and year by year.

Then about ten years ago I got f—ed out of a great job and with that came time, boredom, bitterness and despair. You became my constant companion. I lost my drive and desire for life. My lust for life dwindled, I still loved my wife and children more than ever, but as they recognized my increasing dependence on your daily visits and earlier starting times when we would meet, they began pointing out that our relationship was becoming unhealthy. I got angry, resentful and deceitful. As my personal relationships deteriorated to the point that even I began to see how physically, mentally and personal our relationship had totally become, it was too late for me to just stop seeing you. Sure I made half-assed promises to quit seeing you, made appearances at support groups, but I never bought into the god thing. I would tell the family that I was going to a meeting, sit in my car with a book and you by my side in a parking lot. I'd return home, tell everyone what a great meeting it had been and then you and I would continue our relationship into the night after they all went to bed.

After you cost me my first DUI the luster was gone, my marriage was over and the respect from my children was non-existent. My very freedom is now in jeopardy. I put together three months being away from you, but the loneliness, guilt, despair and self-loathing and helplessness and hopelessness has driven me back to you. I attempted suicide but a K-9 and helicopter saved me from you.

Well my dear this is goodbye. Not see ya later, not maybe in a year or so. You have cost me everything in my life that was important to me. Thankfully my wife and I are civil and my children still love me. Maybe in time I can earn back the respect from my friends and family. As far as I'm concerned our love affair is over never to be revisited. Love has turned to hate. This hate will never be changed by your serene song and whispers of tranquility.

The whole man is impacted and held captive under the guise of love and the illusion of harmony. Randy has offered a glimpse into that world, that relationship, and the void that was ripped open rather than the promised serenity.

Robert illustrates a simple thought or wish for choice and change through these three heartfelt poems:

Poem 1

The world turns and turns

My heart burns and yearns

For a bigger meaning...a higher purpose

I feel like I'm cheating..so how do I serve this...

Earth in the best way that I can

I feel a re-birth at hand

But I think I just need to birth the plan

I scan the skies and study the land

..around me

Trying to think profoundly

Not at all sleeping soundly

Trying to reminisce proudly

But it's hard and many parts are cloudy

Body's tired but mind is rowdy...

with contemplation's

It's not in me to be complacent

Remaining..trying to be patient

Poem 2

Stuck in the asylum of my own head

Can't seem to change, it's how I was bred

Try to be positive, but addicted to dread

Straining to break free of these chains that bind

Hopefully waiting for some kind of sign

Stupidly thinking that it will just happen

Increasingly closer to completely snapping

I try to look in the mirror,

but the glass just keeps cracking

Wishing the answers were on a page in front of me

Knowing the answers won't be something I can see...

But will come from within

How do I attain the key to unlock this grid

Uncork the bottle to a limitless elixir

Caught up short every time in this twister

Shot up forth from within this abyssal

Poem 3

Mind is restless, thoughts are racing

Time seems endless if you're pacing

But it seems I've been living at a sprint...

Thinking of things I've done.. I wince

Wishing to see clearly but everything's in tints

So I try to clear the air with these prints...

But sometimes I fear to care about my stints

I swear I near an epiphany

Trying to cause one continually

Alas...it's not something you can force

I need to deal and let go of my remorse

Constantly debating like the waving of the shores

Constantly aching like a million sores...

But I cope because that's all I can do

Pray and hope to get through...

but in the right way

Constantly contradicting...

It's what I call my night and day

Roberts's inner world is blistered and shredded by many years of addiction. His hopes and longings are captured beautifully in his line *I swear I near an epiphany.* His, like so many others, is a persistent and repetitive push towards reconciliation of thought, emotion, and decision. His writing, an exercise of hopefulness and prayer offers perhaps to no one but himself, a modest benediction.

One day I had arrived to my office and as I opened the door, like many unplanned conversations, I found that someone had slipped this Goodbye poem under it for me to see and read. Although its' author is unknown, its' message is one of universality among the addicted .

Goodbye Forever I hope

Why does it affect me this bad?

What you've done to me is wrong

The goals I had in life are ruined by you and it's not fair,

My dreams as a child were destroyed

You have taken my family away from me and I still adore you

It was all about having fun in the beginning, but then came

A time when I needed you in my life, then you were not there,

All alone again

I found ways and means to let you back into my life again and you let me down.

I lost the trust of my girlfriend, friends, employers, my freedom and happiness.

The feeling of being useful in my life has vanished.

Why should I trust you again.

After being in 8 to 10 detoxes, locked up in hospitals, programs

I still trust you....

No..It's time for me to move on

Start my life again...without you....

What you are to me is nothing but no good

and it's time for me to say goodbye forever..I hope!!

The unparalleled and unmitigated hopes which are deeply echoed here, the wish for health and happiness, the candid recognition of days gone are a vital and truthful allegory representative of so many men. Possibilities however, continue to reverberate with sluggish courage and fraught optimism.

Here, Aaron's poem aptly titled fully expresses this:

Goodbye Poem

You have given me so much pleasure

You have caused me so much pain

You didn't warn me about what I was getting myself into

I had no idea of everything I would be throwing away

When I picked you up that day

Eventually I had to go to court

My family was there with no support

Because I had taken all their trust

My friends didn't like the choices I made

Taking stuff from stores I paid the price

But soon I turned myself around

Put the nasty drug that I found

In the trash and walked away

And as time flew by without getting high

My life grew better everyday

Goodbye -

Part IV
Additional Thoughts

The methodology by which we, as a substance abuse/dependence and prevention industry, use in an attempt to assist men and women whose addictions have taken over their lives is characterized in part by the term *detoxification factories.* The cyclical nature of addiction and the high costs typically incurred both on a community/state level and a regional and federal level make it a multi-billion-dollar industry. In fact one could easily pay upward of $50,000 a month to be treated at a so-called high-end or luxury treatment facility with a daily massage, a dip in a nice pool, and exercise in the ultramodern gym, only to complete the program and be back on the street looking feverishly for a drug and out a lot of money for a nice time in paradise.

Sadly, the millions of dollars that get spent on agencies and residential facilities in a valiant effort to help save lives have forced these programs to put limits on care and placements: hence, the term *factories.* In many cases, there has been a tremendous departure from what would be considered a strong inpatient policy, such as a thirty-day commitment, perhaps court mandated, which was the foundational structure of my facility, down to our current seventeen to possibly a meager twelve- or thirteen-day stay. These have literally been converted into production centers governed essentially by insurance companies who cover the costs for the services rendered (a necessary evil and a true benefit).

New insurance practices have already placed lifetime limits on the number of detoxes they will reimburse. The desperate and street-bound addict or alcohol-dependent person will not have the coverage and will have to rely self

-pay options or on the generosity of a kind benefactor.

Statistics favor and repeatedly demonstrate the efficacy of longer inpatient stays to the tune of months, not days or weeks, and those facilities that support strong, structured programs. Often, the focus turns to time onsite versus quality of care and services rendered as a result of unfortunate cost factors, very real factors indeed and ones that can't be avoided any way one slices the proverbial money pie. Often our ability to provide quality care: to address the psycho-social, spiritual, and badly damaged biological needs of the addicted person, our neighbors, gets profoundly dampened, hampered by the consequences of the economy.

Our system of treatment has become an assembly line or a cookie-cutter model, certainly among the publicly funded agencies and most nonprofits, as the service industry attempts to scrape together enough funding to maintain medical, mental health, and aftercare solutions, solutions that are a staple of the overall needs that will lie in wait until the next time around for many of these men.

We have a tendency to favor treatment of drug addiction with more drugs. The irony here is that it becomes medically necessary to manage life-threatening withdrawal symptoms with medication. Some of these medications are themselves highly addictive and yet somehow they are viewed as better than the alternative. In some cases, in fact, they are. Suboxone, for example, is a synthetic opiate called an opioid used as a replacement therapy. The synthetic opioid is better than the actual opiate—heroin, Percocet, etc.—because it is dispensed under the care of a doctor. It is, however, still a drug that is highly habit forming. Much safer also because it prevents one from seeking drugs on the street, which is not only a dangerous situation but also an unpredictable one, as well as an illegal activity that can put someone, maybe a mother or a son, in jail or in physical harm.

In any case, there is a clear—or not so clear, need for a

radical shift in the approach of the addicted individual and the addicted brain. As of this writing, there are some fundamental steps or treatment goals that have been recognized as basic guidelines to increase the chances for a successful recovery, or at least management of, addictive tendencies and behaviors, ultimately gaining control over the patient's actions and choosing's.

Initially, there is a safe, medical, detoxification process, during which there is a total abstinence from all choice substances, which is mandatory. This is done using various medications to protect an individual from potentially life-threatening and unquestionably uncomfortable withdrawal symptoms. Next is the process of addressing the underlying psychiatric or comorbid mental health concerns, such as depression, anxiety, or history of trauma, with a qualified health care and mental health professional. Usually, this process is followed by a continuum of care after treatment in the facility has concluded. It is important to include identifying and learning how to avoid triggers: those people, places, and things that generate a craving and a subtle reminder often leading to relapse and learning how to manage expectations in early recovery, a one to two year period of time.

This is a scary process for many, as it involves looking deeply at one's life and the circumstances that have led them there, to that very moment in the first place: facing an impending divorce, the death of a loved one, (even if it was fifteen years earlier), or losing one's job, is frightening and debilitating for many. It shuts people down, rendering them helpless, unable to move in life. This is followed by the development of a significant support system, which includes adopting a lifestyle that is centered on sober living and identifying people who can be there when one is feeling the need to obtain their drug once again.

These are all basic, fundamental, and well-researched, evidenced-based strategies developed by top therapists and medical professionals in the field for leading one into a healthy way of being without the use of drugs. However, medical and psychosocial interventions for facilitating well-being, such as counseling, psychoactive medications, and even support networks, tend to be highly operator-dependent, meaning that they assume an individual is able to think and process enough valuable information, especially through the counseling process, to allow the individual to become proactive and to be able to break free from deeply embedded habits and memory systems to maintain focus and motivation.

Brain regions that have been hijacked, taken over by abused drugs, are typically those brain sections that initiate motivation and provide a moral compass. As a consequence, I believe there is a pressing need for interventions that act through the brain itself as command central and shaper of behavioral outputs.

These men earnestly, intentionally attempt to follow through with treatment plans designed to apply the above prescribed ingredients that ideally should lead them back from a progressively disorganized personality and progressive social dysfunction to a more stable and predictable living. However, what the statistics demonstrate is that this approach really doesn't work to the degree that we would like it to.

It seems logical and realistic, and yet there is a crucial piece missing, or perhaps overlooked, that may be required for the mixture to be just right: the way in which brain creates mind. The physical brain is programmed for survival and yet we have a mind constructed to posit meaning and association for everyday life which appears to be disconnected from the addicted person's sense of choice, often leading to disastrous consequences.

***

Antonio Damasio, professor of neuroscience, psychology,

and neurology and the author of *Self Comes to Mind*, ponders the differences between the conscious mind and the unconscious processes of the activities within the brainstem. He suggests that early life forms didn't require a conscious, subjective mind, one alive, endowed with the qualities of self we spoke of earlier, which can predict and project someone into a future state or recall and reflect upon a past experience, because those processes were unnecessary for the survival of life at the time.

The addicted brain, as well, is merely operating in an objective or unconscious and patternistic way, as we have seen, as the brain's reward system kicks in to drive urges and compulsions. Addictions override newer brain systems that generate or construct our values, judgments, and morality. In such a state, executive decision–making skills are compromised much like the residual and debilitating effects of trauma.

The brain gets stuck in looped patterns of behavior or functioning that, although may help the brain to *feel* okay, safe for another day of living in its own brain time moment, ultimately become corrosive to the body as a whole. Traumatologists, neurologists, neurophysiologists, and others in the field of brain disorders and trauma are discovering the devastating and ultimately destructive influence of these stuck patterns of brain systems.

Fibromyalgia, some forms of arthritis, digestive disorders such as Crohn's disease, irritable bowel syndrome along with, sleep disorders, chronic pain disorders, problems concerning memory, and others may be the physical or manifest reaction to these stuck patterns. Harmful biological processes such as the stress hormone cortisol that is used to assist and direct our bodies to protect us in times of stress causes much harm when there is prolonged production without any real and immediate threat. A good example of this is the shrinking of the hippocampus which has a direct and lasting effect on memory.

What is beginning to be understood about the brain is that, in its exquisite complexity and with all of its neural connections, perhaps on the order of five hundred billion neurons and numbers possibly in the trillions of synaptic connections, it is generating electrical fields called frequencies. There may be upward of fifty thousand of these frequencies, all responsible for some manner of our deeply personal *being*. Yes, the three and a half pounds of neural webbing activates across an amazing array of rhythms or frequencies, cycling at a wide range of rhythms. These rhythms appear to be the stuff of mind—our cognitive presence, all of our mental activity and thus, our behavior.

"In many ways, the rhythmic functionality of the brain encourages us to think of it as a most wonderful musical instrument," says Lee Gerdes, author of *Limitless You*, founder of Brainstate Technologies, and developer of a process known as Brainwave Optimization (BWO), scientifically known as (HIRREM) high-resolution relational electroencephalographic mirroring. Brainwave Optimization facilitates the brain's adjustment of its own brainwave activity, in order to balance and optimize itself by using an acoustic mirror or mirror of sound. Theoretically, the brain looks at its own reflection and adjusts itself toward balance or healing. "The brain un-sticks itself by observing itself, much like you or I straightening our hair on a windy day after seeing our messed-up hair in the bathroom mirror." says Gerdes.

To extend the analogy, Gerdes says, "the owner of a brain is like a musician. And the lives we create for ourselves, are like so many pieces of musical art. What happens when a musical instrument strikes a hard surface? Often, its tuning can be disturbed. When an instrument becomes de-tuned, the music will be off, no matter how skilled the musician."

When young men and women experience trauma or repeated feelings of helplessness due to their unfortunate and deeply intrusive circumstances, the brain's rhythms become disturbed and stuck—not unlike a de-tuned musical instrument, similar to what we see in the addicted person. The brain calculates and guesses about the outside world from its massive data supply given by our senses and our experiences, and directs the inside world—our body, to do something to ensure its survival.

An extreme example of this can be seen as Jason and his twin brother dissociate due to horrific experiences. We can perhaps think of their brains as creating rhythms so very different to the extreme, so incredibly unique that we simply cannot recognized them: a raw adaptation, an extreme evolutionary tactic, strictly for survival.

***

As a provider of Brainwave Optimization, as well as being a practicing psychotherapist, I have seen just how trauma affects brain rhythms and the autonomic nervous system in a most direct and dramatic way. Men and women who use this process will typically have an overabundance of various *ranges* of frequencies in the temporal lobes, above the ears and the frontal regions of the brain (pre-frontal cortex), the forehead area. When these areas of the brain are reflected back to themselves, the brain has a tendency to calm or quiet itself. As this calming occurs, the patient's internal experience—the ability to feel emotion without becoming overwhelmed, to focus attention, and to interact with people across many situations without getting triggered, greatly improves.

The human brain is a magical, enchanting and dynamic organ, one that has the capacity to build great cities, evolve religions, create beautiful music, and generate language systems for communicating with other brains. It also has the capacity to create truth then manipulate that truth and destroy itself in the process. A poetic irony and a profound paradox.

In his very intriguing and wonderful book *Phantoms in the Brain*, V. S. Ramachandran describes the cruelty of phantom limb syndrome. A man who lost his arm as it was being crushed continued to experience pain in that arm, even though it no longer existed in physical reality. When the arm was crushed, his fist had been frozen in a clenched position as a reflexive reaction to that pain. Ramachandran, and his team, devised a mirror box in which this person would place his existing arm with a clenched hand. When the patient looked into the box, his brain observed the arm that had been severed in the reflection. The patient was then directed to open his clenched hand, and within moments reported that the pain just dissolved. The brain had been deliberately deceived. It observed two arms when looking into that mirror and theoretically received the feedback it needed to generate a decision that could go something like "Ah, there it is, I've been waiting for new information." A remarkable discovery for Ramachandran and his team and of course the patient.

I tell this story to illustrate how the brain merely takes in and collects data from a variety of sources: in this case, from the eyes. It then interprets that information into something meaningful in order to direct the flow of energy throughout the body. The eyes sent a signal to the brain that "ah... there's the arm, and the hand...,ah...it is now relaxed," in effect, causing the brain to stop *thinking* erroneously that the hand continued to be clenched and in pain. It was shown this through a simple reflection similar to the process of BWO as mentioned above.

It seems so simple, and yet this is only one of many possible methods or strategies to communicate with the brain, as strange as all this sounds. That we even need a way, a system to communicate with something that seems like ours in the first place. It's as if we're trying to communicate with a different life form. Well, maybe we are, to some extent. We communicate with the organic matter of the brain using chemistry and electricity all the time.

The use of antidepressants, antipsychotic or antianxiety medications is a communication which takes place through chemical bonding. We send the brain messages through relaxation, deep breathing exercises, and electroconvulsive therapy (ECT) as well. Messages and commands are constantly on the go throughout the entire body complex, but direct communication with the brain is a challenge. Many talented and dedicated professionals are working on ways to cause communication to happen to help resolve many debilitating conditions.

There are the many variations of the trauma / addiction cycle and their insidious and disruptive effects. From the unfortunate, sad, and dissociative collapse of the fragile psyches of two desperate brothers trying to survive the brutality of a mother's scorn, to phantom limbs, and the brain's inclination toward routine or pattern making, creating maps with which to delineate tasks throughout our anatomy. The brain simply wants responses to its inquiries. It is constantly looking for feedback to help guide it and inform it. In addiction and trauma, this is what we want, answers or feedback in support of health, happiness and stability.

Part V

Strategies For Wellness

Over the past fifteen years or so, there have risen dozens of "alternative" strategies for healing and promoting wellness through the use of very interesting techniques. Here I use the term alternative to indicate any healing modality, which may appear to be seen by some, as substandard and grossly at odds with what we commonly refer to as *traditional western medicine.*

Traditional Western medicine is what we typically expect to receive when we visit with our doctor. We hope to be seen and examined, and through the process, to be assured of a diagnosis and a hopeful treatment. Mostly, treatments assume that there is indeed a cure for what ails us. A quick, and simple cure, like taking an antibiotic or pain medication.

Often, pain reduction is the most that one can hope for, especially for *traumatic pain:* pain which is not easily seen, or measurable, and therefore frequently dismissed, and minimized to awful consequences and lifelong misery. Too often, the pain relief comes at the very high price of addiction with the potential source of the pain being left untreated and left to persist. The addiction might be that of drugs, and/or lifestyle. People who experience chronic pain often develop a lifestyle which conforms to their self-imposed limits, as they try their best to deal with terrible discomfort. Staying home too frequently, avoiding situations that may cause a flare-up, restricted by feelings of embarrassment, caused by the experience of "unseen", and "unprovoked", or un-diagnosed symptoms of debilitating pain.

Traumatic pain is that pain caused by undischarged trauma as the person lives each day with a brain and nervous system, which cannot distinguish between the events of the present, and those of the past. There is a constant barrage of false memories locked into the body which need to be updated and discharged.

The discharge I'm speaking of is the chemical, hormonal build -up which the body has generated in order to respond to a perceived or actual threat of harm. Earlier, I've written about panic attacks, how frightening and debilitating they can be: sudden Increases in heart rate, sweating, shakiness and a general feeling of being ill at ease, increased breathing etc, cause significant psychological distress. The same hormones present during the traumatizing event or events, remain fully intact, and at the ready. Those hormones, that internal mechanism, must be discharged so that one feels in control, and no longer threatened, and helpless in the face of fear. Strategies to assist an individual to become whole, and less fearful, are outlined here.

***

Cognitive Behavioral Therapy, simply known as CBT, is the most widely used treatment modality in psychotherapy today. It's a talk therapy, used to guide the patient into an understanding that, how one thinks influences how they feel, and with that, so they respond. It is a profoundly useful technique, widely studied and proven to be effective for most common psychological stress. *Traumatic pain* however does not reside at the level of thought and speaking. It is not generally a cognitive process, but the cognitive process is greatly impacted by it. It is buried within the nerves, small muscles and tendons of the body.

As a result, different strategies have been, and continue to be recognized and developed for their usefulness in assisting and encouraging the body to discharge the stuck patterns of trauma. Aside from Brainwave Optimization which I've described earlier, here I've listed others which I believe can be quite supportive in assisting the body to come into the present, with the full capacity to learn and be imaginative in most fulfilling ways.

The first strategy which comes to mind is an amazing discovery by Dr. David Berceli while working with people after they experience the trauma of natural disaster, war and conflict. Dr. Berceli is the creator of Trauma Releasing Exercises or TRE. He noticed that mammals have an innate tendency to shake or display tremoring after being involved in a dangerous situation where vast expenditures of hormones were released into the body. People, he observed, also did this but not as readily. Often culture, and other social constraints, force people to hide or mask these natural release mechanisms. This prevents the trauma from escaping, from being burned off or discharged. Trauma releasing exercises, are exercise that assist the body in releasing "deep muscular patterns of stress, tension and trauma", which get locked into the body and remembered. Trauma Releasing Exercises "activate a natural reflex mechanism of shaking or vibrating that releases muscular tension, calming down the nervous system. "When this muscular shaking/vibrating mechanism is activated, in a safe and controlled environment, says Berceli, the body is encouraged to return back to a state of balance".

Yoga is another releasing mechanism which can assist the body in returning to a state of balance by discharging the tension buried within. Yoga literally means union with self. As the postures and breath-work are routinely practiced, one is better able to unconsciously dissolve the stuck patterns of false memories. This is accomplished by intentionally tuning in to separate muscle groups, and becoming more mentally focused on areas within the body which appear more ridged and prone to pain. Since trauma, as I've discussed it here is fundamentally a dissociative state or experience, one which perpetuates past somatic responses, the practice of yoga brings one back to a reality based in current time and place. Meditation is also a part of the tradition of yoga.

Through the practice of meditation one learns to focus on the breath, or a mantra (simple encouraging phrase) or some other fixed point, in order to remain unattached to the myriad thoughts which can be overwhelming and distracting. It's a practice which can help one to constantly remember to be here... now, in the present. Most of our day is spent thinking about the future or remembering, and living in the past. Meditation can help return us to the Now, restore our sense of being, our enduring sense of self to the moment at hand. It requires some effort to shape the environment and prepare to sit comfortably for ten minutes or longer. This is a practice which is to be repeated daily and built into a routine. The only goal is to practice becoming mindful, self-aware and to become reacquainted with one's bodily feelings and sensations as they occur.

Moving into more therapeutic and highly specialized treatments which require professional involvement, eye movement desensitization and reprocessing or EMDR as it is commonly known, is a form of psychotherapy which uses eye movements to assist clients in processing distressing memories and beliefs. Like the trauma releasing exercises, EMDR is thought of as a natural method to help the body discharge tension brought about by trauma through a combination of specific eye movements and the remembering / re-telling of traumatic memories. It is an exposure therapy, meaning that the individual is brought back to the time of the threatening experience to help reformulate the physiological arousal associated with trauma. This process has also been well studied and offers strong efficacy outcomes.

Emotional Freedom Techniques known as EFT and Tapping is another option which requires minimal training initially, but to get into the deeper aspects of traumatic healing would require someone with professional, experiential training. This is a tool which has been found to be very useful in bringing relief to many who have suffered from ptsd and traumatic pain as well. As with EMDR, CBT, Yoga, and Meditation, EFT has been well studied and found to be quite powerful in restoring emotional health and vitality. This technique combines the 5000 year history of Acupuncture with traditional therapy. Acupuncture, (used with needles), and Acupressure, (applied without needles but, instead, uses finger pressure), directly uses the energy meridians of the body to release what is thought of as "blocked" energy systems. It is thought that all emotional disharmony is regulated by these meridians. Through Tapping on various places on the body and mentally "tuning in" to specific issues, these "energy blockages" can be released. As the release is happening, there is a re-structuring of networks of *energy* throughout the body to increase blood flow and healthy unrestricted patterns of functioning. In effect, allowing for physical, cognitive, and emotional well-being.

We are currently on the precipice in technological advances to be able to measure these energy systems. In fact, Konstantin Korotkov a professor of Physics at St. Petersburg National Research University of Informational Technologies, Mechanics and Optics in Russia and a senior researcher at St. Petersburg Research institute of Physical Culture has been observing and measuring these systems for many years. Through his work and the esteemed works of many other dedicated researchers, validation of the strategies mentioned and their mechanisms for promoting change is beginning to emerge with much more enthusiasm, acceptance and tolerance throughout the medical community.

The Boy in the Chicken Coop

Conclusion

Trauma and addiction are both conditioned responses to fear; hijacking brain structures and functionality along the way, which have a profound effect on the physiological, cognitive, and emotional systems of the body, as well as the very structure of the brain itself.   They create a system of autonomic dysregulation. Although their beginnings may be quite unique, differentiated by the encounter, experience and meaning; they share the common outcome of helplessness in the face of threat. One, the threat of personal bodily harm, possible life or death; and, the other, the threat of physical discomfort. Both are a violation of personal safety.

Although trauma always starts out as an actual threat in the face of helplessness as a single, or prolonged event, addiction often begins as an act of innocence, medical,or psychological necessity. They both however share the common traits of suffering and an overwhelming internal experience which often include: intrusive thoughts, feelings and physical disharmony.

One key difference between everyday negative life events and traumatic events is the implication of procedural memory, which records *all* of the body's *reactions* to trauma, somatic renderings, during the time of the actual events. The clenched teeth, the tightened neck muscles, the sick feeling in the gut prior to getting abused or hit by the car or operated on for the removal of the bladder. Procedural memories differ from our everyday memories of the immediate need to recall the grocery list or paying the bills after calling the veterinarian and are referred to as explicit memory.

Explicit memory helps us learn and function on our day to day activities where conscious thought and control are necessary for survival. Procedural memory or implicit memory are a set of fixed memories which had been used to learn how to ride a bike for example or play tennis. Initially one is very much aware of each step involved in placing ones foot on the peddle or hand position on the racket. After a while, and with practice, we learn and no longer must *think* about how to do these things. Learned behavior is procedural memory. It becomes an inherent act without the requirement of a conscious observer.

In trauma, procedural memories serve as a warning system to the body, but have lost their sense of time in the present. They reflect the exact muscle patterns and sensations during the traumatizing event. They live in the past and have not yet been discharged or updated to reflect factual, in the now activities of daily life. They continue to be played out during activities of the present, which may simply suggest a similarity to the feelings of threat which were present during the traumatic events. Getting screamed at or being in a room full of strangers can quite easily turn into a re-experiencing of the same physical symptoms just as one experienced them at an earlier time in life when an actual threat was happening. Cues can rise from any experience both, from around us, and from within, causing panic and great fear.

As time and technology expand our awareness of the body and its' natural states, along with its' very curious mechanisms for both, the erosion of physical and emotional health, and the healing from that erosion, we continue to learn from the many researchers and observers alike who specialize in the healing arts.

In the final analysis, says visionary, poet, and peace ambassador James O'Dea, the former Washington office director of Amnesty International and author of *Creative Stress*, "All the ligaments and tendons of the social body, community and the fragile structure of the 'self' are woven together to form the unity of belonging and placement into this larger global connection...this living being."

***

And so with those thoughtful words, I leave you, the reader, with this simple question:

How does one learn to embrace their vulnerabilities, imperfections, and personal history, so that they can engage in life, this social body, from a place of authenticity and worthiness? How do we help cultivate the courage, compassion, and connection that we all need to recognize that we are enough—that we are worthy of love, belonging, and joy?

References

Damasio, Antonio 2010. *Self Comes to Mind*

Gerdes, Lee 2008. *Limitless You Namaste Publishing*

Gorski, Terence: *Various readings*

Journal of the National Library of Addictions. *May 2011*

Kandel, Eric 2006. *In Search of Memory.*

Levine, Peter A., Kline, Maggie 2007. *Trauma Through a Child's Eyes.* North Atlantic Books

Levine, Peter A 1997. *Waking the Tiger: Healing Trauma.*

O'Dea, James 2010. *Creative Stress*

Porges, Stephen 2011. *The Polyvagal Theory*

Ramachandran, V. S 2011. *The Tell-Tale Brain.* Norton

Ramachandran, V. S 2004. *A Brief Tour of Human Consciousness.* PI Press

Sacks, Oliver 1989. *Seeing Voices.* Vintage Books

Scaer, Robert 2007. *The Body Bears the Burden (Trauma, Dissociation and Disease).* Sec. Ed. Routledge

Shermer, Michael 2011. *The Believing Brain.* Times Books

Vygotsky, L. S 1962. *Thought and Language.* MIT Press

Selected Reading

Trauma Releasing Exercises	David Berceli
The Believing Brain	Michael Shermer
Phantoms in the Brain	V. S. Ramachandran
The Tell-Tale Brain	V. S. Ramachandran
The Mind's Eye	Oliver Sacks
The River Of Consciousness	Oliver Sacks
Seeing Voices	Oliver Sacks
An Anthropologist on Mars	Oliver Sacks
Creative Stress	James O'Dea
The Body Bears the Burden	Robert Scaer
The Trauma Spectrum	Robert Scaer
In Search of Memory	Eric Kendel
Self Comes to Mind	Antonio Damasio
The Energy of Health	Konstantin Korotkov

ABOUT THE AUTHOR

Steven B. Sherman, Licensed Mental Health Counselor, is a practicing psychotherapist and the Owner /Director of Central Massachusetts Brain Integration Center [2010 - 2015]. For over twenty-five years, Steve has worked in the field of human services and has dedicated his study to broadening his understanding of the human condition. His career includes working with adults on the autism spectrum, work on a suicide hot-line, work in the fields of addiction, and brainwave-analysis using a process known as Brainwave Optimization.

As a psychotherapist, Steve is able to observe the behavioral, physiological, and psychological symptoms of trauma and addiction as they are expressed by his many patients. As the Owner / Director of Central Massachusetts Brain Integration Center Steve has been able to observe individual brainwave frequency patterns utilizing electroencephalogram technology or EEG, combined with computer analysis, both of which appeared to correlate to significant emotional distress by the patients he served.

Combining his years of practical and diverse experiences, Steve's work at the Men's Addiction Treatment Center, a Section 35 civil commitment center for men with significant drug and alcohol dependency issues for 5 years, has brought to bear his current book *"The Boy in the Chicken Coop."*